Home
From Home

artwork: ben willis, www.whitenoisestudios.com

A note from me,

There is so much I could say, but this bookazine isn't about me. In fact it isn't really about homes - it's about Jesus and vibrant Christian living within four walls.

I was a freelance interior stylist and writer for a number of glossies and got to view some jaw-dropping houses. Maybe I am just plain old nosy, but I love to have a good look around other people's property. You only have to take a quick glance at any magazine stand to see people's fascination with anything bricks and mortar.

Speaking from personal experience, I know that a nice house isn't always a nice home. My last house was in the glossies, but beyond the swanky furniture and designer labels my life was in ruins. It was a great looking house but as dead and cold as a morgue.

Behind closed doors I returned to my daily crisis. Heart-ache: I'd been there, seen it, done it, worn the t-shirt. Believe me I could write a book. The reality was that the house was one of many masks that I hid behind.

I didn't know then what I know now - consuming love, Jesus love. How wide & long & high & deep is the love of Christ!

My heart is that the pages of this bookazine would both encourage and inspire you. I trust God will make a way for this bookazine to be on many coffee tables. How exciting to be able to tell others of the love of God in this way.

As the editor, author and a recovering dyslexic, I have had a bumpy ride in uncharted waters. Praise God He calms the storm!

I have shared with you my heart, so now Samuel my husband and I share with you our home.

So go on, kick off your shoes, grab a cuppa and indulge yourself in a large piece of chocolate cake.

Joint restoration

I met the real Jesus in the gutter. That's where I was and that's where he met me. I was at the end of the line and that was the beginning of a great new journey with Him. In the middle of all my chaos and the storm of my mind I met Love, I met Jesus, I met peace.

The words from Psalm 139 saved me literally from the brink.

O Lord, you have searched me and you know me. You know when I sit and when I rise; you perceive my thoughts from afar echoed in my mind. He knew, He understood and He cared!

A local property agent approached me about buying an old house - he knew I was a serial renovator. The house needed lots of TLC - what he didn't know was that so did I! I completed on the property and took a huge gulp. The keys opened the door for a joint restoration.

Everyday God spoke to me through the tasks performed in the renovation. As each room was stripped of layers of paper, He gently peeled away the layers of confusion in my mind. Cracks and crumbling plaster were exposed, as were all the lies I had believed about myself. Wires, pipes, boards and windows were replaced and the lies were blotted out by truth, His Word. There were lights, warmth, water and fresh plaster. The shell now had life and so did I! Flourishing in shalom peace - nothing missing, nothing broken, I painted each wall.

Sam & Talitha

Whitehead Bay

A treasure chest

The early 1900's house was a gem: so many original features including cornicing, stained glass windows, solid panelled doors, fireplaces and servant bells. The down side was the drooping ceilings, cracked walls, old faulty wiring, lead pipes and no central heating. With sheer determination, a sledge-hammer and a crow bar work began. At one point in the renovation you could stand on the ground floor and see the slates on the roof. It was gruelling work and I spent months stripping out and I filled 13 Builders skips.

Self-discovery

Once all the hard work had been done, the whole house was painted white - a blank canvas to unleash my creativity - a far cry from my days of samples and tester paints galore. Each room evolved and was inspired by the Bible, prayer and worship. I was determined that I was going to have fun, and fun is what I had and that's when I met Samuel, now my husband. Colour, life and individuality were a must and I made a conscious choice not to play safe and paint the house neutral tones. The whole house is woven together like a tapestry. From the moment you walk through the door and step onto the stripped floors your senses are awakened; it's like a gallery.

photography: michael taylor - www.mtphoto.co.uk

9 Colours in harmony

The downstairs lounge is vibrant; 9 colours are blended together in harmony providing a brilliant backdrop for modern black leather furniture. Circles are integrated in the bold fabric, lighting, cushions and mirrors. Light and colour bounce off the walls.

Kings Road

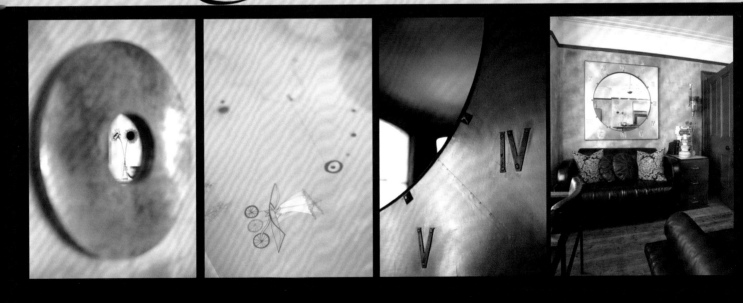

the preachers house

A place to feast
The dining room walls are pasted with pages of prayers, music, cards, carefully hidden love letters and poems. Splashes of translucent colour glazes give a mystical glow; there is a sense of calming rhythm in this room.

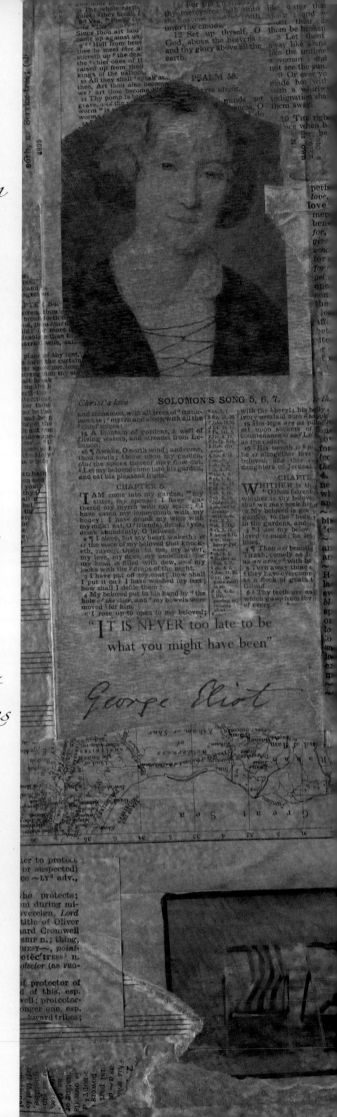

"IT IS NEVER too late to be what you might have been"

George Eliot

An old church pew and a mix of antique and reproduction furniture, rich fabrics and a cast iron fireplace complement the walls.

Here I am! I stand at the door and knock. If anyone hears my voice and opens the door, I will come in and eat with him, and he with me.

Rev 3:20

Smile and unashamedly eat

An Italian slate floor welcomes you as you enter this unique kitchen and eating area. Stone worktops crown the open plan cupboards.

These rooms are light, airy, and incredibly eccentric - one can only smile and feel at ease in this open space. The Smeg stove and fridge say modern living; a leather sofa offers a place to chill. Railway sleepers allow a chaotic order for books; artwork scatters the distressed walls and a retro clock ticks by the back door leading to the courtyard.

I love the exposed pipes, they give an industrial feel to the open space. For some strange reason we have paper clips hanging from our candles. A very cheap way to accessorise.

My friends laughed when I arrived home excited about the old Belfast sink. They said it looked like a pig's trough – now they are eating their words!

Sam and I love to walk, pray and scout for our treasures along the Antrim coast. A glass dish displays our driftwood, smoothed glass, broken pottery and shells.

We used old railway sleepers held by metal braces to support wooden shelves. A white glaze was used to jazz them up. They look great and were very cheap to build.

Mr. untidy was designated his very own vitamin cupboard. Letters from a hardware store were just the job.

I love my coat so much it's become a piece of art on our back door.

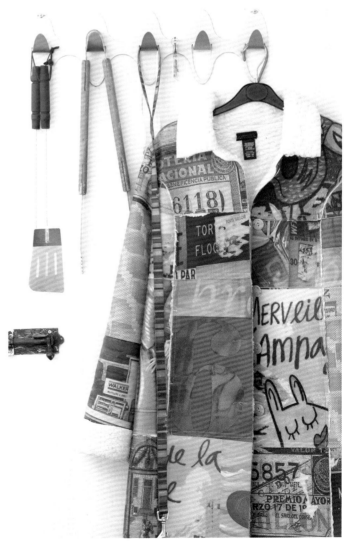

A place to escape

Painted bamboo walls and a starfish splash-back are home to reconditioned bath-ware. The alternative surroundings are a tranquil setting. The full Hessian and velvet curtains sit comfortably along side the old dentist trolley and mirrored wall unit. An original chandelier shadows the walls, scented soaps and perfumes make for a relaxing bathing experience. Bathing here feels like you are away on holiday in some tropical seaside get-away.

Sweet sleep

The bedrooms are to be lived in; each has a place to sit, pray and think in peace.

Psalm 46:10
Be still
and
know
that
I am God

"*Church bells echo in our prayer room*"

Beautiful curtains frame the 5 large sash windows that look out of the upstairs lounge directly at an old church and palm trees. Colour washed walls, an original fireplace and lighting set the stage for large furniture, a love seat and velvet throws. Room is filled with the sound of singing and bells. It has a refreshing and mesmerising feel of escapism into reality and peace.

Spa bath

The large second bathroom is like a spa with a re-upholstered antique chair and an original fireplace that's decorated with locally collected driftwood and shells. The metallic wall tiles reflect the café lighting. Candles, combinations of coppers, golds and earth tones tantalise the eyes. An antique pot stand is filled with shells and demands the same attention as the reproduction bath-ware and mesh screen.

Original crystal chandeliers, fireplaces and large beds with silk throws create a tranquil space. Pale colour washed walls and crisp bedding are contrasted with strong rich colours and pearl glazes. Carefully chosen fabrics, cushions, art and accessories complement the lavish surroundings

MILING INSIDE

ad convinced my husband to put on a facemask,
th that the doorbell rang and a friend called for tea!
ey were still welcome.
anding in our frumpy jim-jams,
aughed, Samuel laughed, they laughed and tea we had.
this time our masks were cracking which made it all the funnier.
e make the house Living Stones.
is a vessel to be used to show love - Jesus love.

mans 8:38
r I am persuaded beyond doubt
m sure) that neither death nor life,
r angels nor principalities,
r things impending and threatening,
r things to come,
r powers,
r height,
r depth,
r anything else
all creation will be able
separate us from
e love of God
hich is in Christ Jesus our Lord.

Corinthians 13:1
nd now I will show you the most excellent way.
I speak in the tongues of men and of angels, but have not love,
am only a resounding gong or a clanging cymbal. If I have the gift of
rophecy and can fathom all the mysteries
nd all knowledge, and if I have the faith that can
ove mountains, but have not love,
am nothing.
I give all I possess to the poor and surrender my body to the flames,
ut have not love, I gain nothing.
ove is patient, love is kind, it does not envy, it does not
oast, it is not proud.
is not rude, it is not self-seeking,
is not easily angered, it keeps no record of wrongs.
ove does not delight in evil but rejoices with truth.
always protects, always trusts,
lways hopes, always perseveres.

Love never fails

"I have a passion for good coffee shops and tearooms ..."

... there is something about the buzz – the noise of chit-chat and laughter as people just hang out and enjoy being together in a relaxed environment.

Don't get me wrong! I still put the kettle on at home. I enjoy a pot of hot tea, curled up in a comfy armchair in front of an open fire. Since marrying a Northern Irish man my skills for making a good brew have developed. Now after making a pot of tea, I put it on the stove – giving extra time to brew at boiling point!

So why am I still enticed into paying someone else for that perfect cuppa? For me there are many ingredients: the freshly ground coffee, cakes and surroundings, combined with a feeling of taking time out with friends – and being away from the housework and laundry might have something to do with it!

I must admit I have become a bit of a coffee snob, and can't bear instant coffee anymore – ummm, I can imagine the smell of freshly ground coffee beans. There is something very comforting about wrapping your hands around a large mug of cappuccino, latte, mochaccino, Americano, steamer, or traditional filter coffee – especially on a cold rainy day. A strong shot of double espresso used to be my favourite, but now I like to savour the whole coffee shop moment.

My husband is a hot chocolate fan and always has a big smile on his face when his mug is overflowing with a big blob of cream and a mountain of marshmallows. If I was to indulge in a hot chocolate, I would have to forgo a piece of cake and that's a big 'no-no!'

Cakes can look so beautiful like artwork to be looked at and admired – almost too good to eat. My taste buds are stirred by home baked chocolate or passion cake with a serving of fresh cream, or chunky, white chocolate and blueberry scones that melt in your mouth.

So many coffee shops have a great selection of global foods. The menu can be so good that your intention for 'just coffee' can be totally wrecked and a short break can lead into an afternoon of feasting!

What with the melodic rhythm of coffee shop music, comfy chairs, café lighting, and walls decorated with art, one could almost be hypnotised into spending more time in the oasis of coffee beans and cake.

With the whole sense of community in mind, I love it that so many churches have caught on. The coffee shop has now become a bridge into life beyond the typical church environment. So now I can have it all – 'The Promised Land' flowing with church, coffee and cake all under one roof – Praise God!

reflection, revelation, restoration

artwork: dermot mcconaghy　design: www.markflint.net

'It's time to fly; it's time to fly; it's time to fly,' I would say to myself.

I have always been captivated by the journey that takes place for butter-flies: from being a caterpillar to a chrysalis, and then, at the right time, it all happens – quickly – like a sudden transformation to utter beauty and freedom! Such wonder, such colour!

In my brokenness I would stand on a cliff with the wind blowing in my face as I looked out at the vastness of the ocean. So many questions would echo in my mind – I felt as if my head was going to explode with the pressure of confusion and pain.

Heartache: I'd been there, done it, worn the t-shirt, believe me at the age of 36, I could write a book including chapters on: miscarriage, barrenness, hysterectomy, menopause, infidelity, divorce, domestic violence, sexual abuse, depression, eating disorders, low self esteem, self hatred, loneli-ness and so on … really the list felt like the abyss!

I knew abuse. I knew church. I knew religion. I knew how to wear a mask, but I didn't know who I was and what I know now: love, Jesus-love. How wide and long and high and deep is the love of Christ!

I was so broken, so deceived, I didn't know where to turn; I would lay on my face for hours, begging God to forgive me, and get up again still condemning myself and still in the spiral of self destruction my life had taken on.

I felt like a misfit that just didn't belong in the world or the Church, as I knew it. All the different denominations and theologies totally confused me.

I spent hours going around in circles: tongues or no tongues, adult dunking or infant baptism, women in ministry or not in ministry, head coverings or no head coverings, music or no music, pre-tribulation or post-tribulation, Calvinist or Armenian? Ahhhhh – my head was hurting!

What was the truth? I wanted it! If I worship using contemporary Christian songs, was I sinning? If I only sang unaccompanied Psalms, was I in bondage? With 3,000 books I still had no answers. I would pick up the Bible and study with a chocolate box mix of perspectives and theology. As a recovering dyslexic, I sat armed with a note pad so I could write down and look up all the words I didn't understand. There were so many I filled a book. This was enough to send anyone over the edge!

I had met the good, the bad and the ugly in every church and every denomination – also passionate mighty men and women of God with such opposing theological views. What if I got the wrong theology? Would I be condemned to hell? The weight was so heavy upon my shoulders.

For years I believed a lie about myself and about God. Finally I couldn't even pick up my Bible. I hated myself – I hated life – I felt like a woman condemned with no escape, even if I sipped death. Everything seemed so grey. I would analyse everything.

As I shared with you earlier in the house article, I sat in the early hours of the morning suicidal on the beach. Drunk and stoned the words from Psalm 139 came to my mind – with such an impact – such reality – such simplicity and set me free:

'O Lord you have searched me and you know me ...'

I had hope; at last I had someone who knew me – someone who cared, someone who could lift the burden from me in His arms of grace, love, forgiveness and give me direction. Jesus would carry me through the splinters of brokenness that had surrounded and engulfed me.

From that moment on – the simplicity of the childlike Word set me free – don't get me wrong it took time to unravel the mess of my life and my mind – like it takes time to become a butterfly, but my spirit was totally whole. I just had to take a step at a time – but I was not alone!

Jesus, who when I was so bowed down and could not get up by myself, met with me and gave me wings to fly! I started to read the Bible again – almost with new, different glasses on.

I saw colour, life and healing in every page I turned to. I found great hope in the words from Luke 13:11-12:

'And behold, there was a woman which had a spirit of infirmity eighteen years, and was bowed together, and could in no wise lift up herself. And when Jesus saw her, He called her to Him, and said unto her, "Woman, thou art loosed from thine infirmity."'

That very same Jesus who met with this woman in the synagogue, who called her to him, met with me. I had been to church for years and had carried infirmities both physical and emotional, and felt like I just couldn't lift myself up. I know many that feel as if they can't get up and break through in their gifting, career, ministry, calling, relationships, finance and so the list goes on. Or they feel like they can't get up in breaking unhealthy feelings, ideas, habits, thoughts about themselves and others, or feel trapped in the cycle of addictions.

But my God, my Jesus, my Ancient of Days, Alpha and Omega, the Beginning and the End, the Resurrection and the Life would say to them as He said to me. 'Woman thou art loosed from thine infirmity.'

I said to myself 'Right, girl! Today is the day to draw a line in the sand. The day to decide to stand up straight, the day to re-align my focus and walk into the fullness of who I am in Jesus and the destiny that He has for me. Today is the day of walking in the reality – 'His yoke is easy and His burden is light.'

Yeah, wow, it was the day! A time of change, like a chrysalis into a beautiful butterfly – It was time to know who I was in Christ and walk in my birthright. It was time to arise as His diadem, His glory, His love made manifest.

I said to myself with gusto, 'I am His voice, His vessel of great worth and purpose. It was time to step into my calling; the Church needs me! The world needs me; it needs Jesus, and I am His hands, His feet and His mouthpiece!'

So I started the journey and His simple Words healed my mind. I often shout aloud spinning around saying, 'Surely Lord you bless the righteous and surround them with your favour as with a shield.' 'Today is my day of metamorphosis, a transforming and a renewing my mind; a time set apart to press on and press in to the heart of my God.'

God spoke to me through His word: 'Forget the former things, do not dwell on the past, see I am doing a new thing!' Today God is meeting us where we are at and saying 'Take my hand!'

I love the scripture in Mark 1:30. Simon's mother-in-law was in bed with a fever, and they told Jesus about her. So he went to her, took her hand and helped her up. The fever left her and she began to wait on them. Today Jesus has come to us; He is taking our hands and is helping us up so that we can go and wait on them, by taking their hands!

There are a number of people in the Bible that had dramatic life changing experiences as they took the hand of Jesus, drew a line in the sand and from that point on walked in their destiny. I have found such encouragement as I have read about them and how they arose!

I love the story of the worldly Samaritan woman at the well in John 4:7. This was a woman who I could relate to – she knew rejection, failure, isolation, shame and heartache. She was a moral outcast who collected water at the hottest part of the day, when she could do so alone. Yet this woman who most people would have written off had a wonderful encounter with Jesus.

How often in our prayers we go all around the houses before we just say it – as if God doesn't know our thoughts and hearts! But Jesus pinpointed her heart issue: 'You have had five husbands and the man you now live with is not your husband.'

She was looking for love. She had a God shaped void – fill me, fix me and make me feel OK. She used other people to help numb her pain, looking for love on all the wrong faces and in all the wrong places, dissatisfied and unfulfilled – but then she met Jesus.

'Sir, give me this water.' And Jesus says to her 'I am He, the Messiah.' He knew her, He loved her and He wanted her true worship!

Wow, what hope! She responded by drawing a line in the sand and leaving the water jar and the mindset and the shame that caused her isolation. She went back to the town and she told them about Jesus. The woman walked in the fullness of the wonderful scripture:

Isaiah 1:18 – 'Though your sins are like scarlet, they shall be as white as snow; though they are red as crimson, they shall be like wool.'

I had the heart of a runaway, but, if she could change, then so could I. So I had to stop wanting to run away, not just physically, but mentally and emotionally in situations, relationships and places.

Again the Word gave me hope that I didn't have to run anymore!

Psalm 84:5,6 – 'Blessed are those whose strength is in you, who have set their hearts on pilgrimage. As they pass through the valley of Baca, they make it a place of springs.'

Baca means weeping – I was now passing through and Jesus was making it my place of springs as I passed through!

Yes! It's wonderful that the woman, the outcast, the misfit, with all her history was then used to lead many of the Samaritans from the town to Jesus! Inside she must have been saying to herself 'No shame here. I'm forgiven. I have met with the Messiah.'

As spoken to the woman at the well, God through His word said to me: 'You may have been looking for love in the wrong places, but: "Whoever drinks the water I give him will never thirst."'

God called me to respond like the Samaritan woman and to leave the jar, the past and all that hindered me, and to go into the town holding my head up high, walking in His righteousness and proclaiming His love.

Next as I searched the scriptures I met with a person of religion and not relationship – of head knowledge, not heart knowledge. Amazing! wonderful! What hope there was as I read Acts 9, Saul's conversion. Here I met a man who was a religious Pharisee and was murdering Christians, but who then had an encounter with Jesus. 'Saul, Saul why do you persecute me?' 'Who are you Lord?' 'I am Jesus, that you are persecuting.'

What a shocking revelation Saul (later known as Paul) had, realising that he was totally sold out to a lie. I had been sold out to a lie: a lie about who God is, and who I was in God. I was sold out to fear and anxiety, and insecurity, and bad unhealthy relationships, and bad habits, and striving and unforgiveness.

Saul obeyed God's command, 'Now get up and go to the city where you will be told what to do.' God chose Ananias to minister His love and spoke to him about Saul, the ex-murderer, and said, 'This man is my chosen instrument to carry my name.'

Love it! I wonder how many people would have picked this man and seen such potential! Ananias lays hands on Saul and he is healed and baptised.

What a response I see from Saul as he draws a line in the sand, and how at once he began to preach in the synagogues that Jesus is the Son of God. In reality so often when we mess up we allow ourselves to become paralysed and inward-looking – but not Saul. He didn't sit for five years beating himself up, instead he shared the revelation of truth that he now had!

There were wagging tongues in Church. It says so in Acts 9:21 – BUT that didn't stop Saul. The Bible says Saul grew more and more powerful! Unfortunately, sometimes even in the church there are wagging tongues – people reminding us of past bad choices.

That didn't stop Saul.

So I decided that it wouldn't stop me – God is my credibility!

To be honest I had many external and internal voices of accusation, but I had to ignore them. I think I was more condemning of myself than anyone else, until I stood in the reality of the Word. I would remind Satan, others and myself, when they tried to pull me down, what the Word of God says:

1 John 1:9 – 'If we confess our sins, he is faithful and just and will forgive us our sins and purify us from all unrighteousness.'

There was a time in my life that I allowed myself to be captive to shame.

One day I wrote on a piece of paper some scripture and the words self-respect and no more shame. I put it in a bag and hung it on the wall in my kitchen.

Every day for two years I reminded myself that Jesus dealt with my shame on the cross.

Every time I wanted to return to a self-pity party and a self-harming lifestyle, I looked at the bag and said to myself 'No more!' By faith I stood in this – the Word – until it became a heartfelt reality.

The reality is we can fly in the truth: Romans 8:31 – 'If God is for us who can be against us!'

Saul (Paul) was fully persuaded of his identity in Jesus and of His eternal love – that's living, eternal living!

Romans 8:38 – 'For I am convinced that neither death nor life, neither angels nor demons, neither the present nor the future, nor any powers, neither height nor depth, nor anything else in all creation, will be able to separate us from the love of God that is in Christ Jesus our Lord.'

'I, Paul, a servant of Christ Jesus called to be an apostle and set apart for the gospel of God'! He knew his calling. He had a past; it was forgiven. He was called and he knew it! Praise God!

Philippians 3:13 – 'Forgetting what is behind and straining towards what is ahead, I press on towards the goal to win the prize for which God has called me heavenwards in Christ Jesus.'

As he stood in the truth and proclaimed the truth, he grew more and more powerful in the Lord. As spoken to Paul, God said to me through His Word: 'I want relationship with you; your past is your past; you are my chosen instrument to carry my name.'

God called me to respond like Paul: to leave being religious and to walk in relationship with Him, rising above what people might say about me.

I am not sure who is my favourite Bible character. Again I can so relate to the next person I read about in Luke 22:31 – Peter. He was a man who had a real and personal relationship with Jesus, but when things came to the crunch, commits a sin that he really didn't think he was capable of.

Jesus knows Peter more than Peter knows himself, and pre-warns him that his actions in time will not match his words – but also offers him hope:

Luke 22:31–34 – 'And when you have turned back strengthen your brothers.'

In Luke 22:54 Peter disowns Jesus, denying that he knew him three times, after publicly saying in verse 33 that he was ready to go with him to prison and to death. Peter's confession didn't match up with his heart – and so the fulfilment of the prophecy took place.

It says that the Lord turned and looked straight at Peter. Christ through His word looked me straight in the eye. How wonderful is our all-knowing God! He knew Peter, really knew Peter, and still loved him. He knew me, really knew me, and He still loved me.

Peter went outside and wept bitterly, and then went back to what he knew. How often when we feel we have failed God do we face the temptation to go back.

But how awesome is our God, who seeks us out! He calls to them, in John 21:4–5, 'Friends, haven't you any fish?' Jesus meets Peter where he is: fishing! Peter had returned to his fishing; I had returned to many things, but Christ hemmed me in.

Psalm 139:7 – 'Where can I go from your presence O Lord?' In John 21:12 Christ pursues him; He cooks him breakfast! God met with Peter in his hunger on the beach, and that's where He met me – in my hunger on the beach!

Christ restored Peter through a three-fold confession, not of belief, but of love, as Jesus asks him three times if he truly loves Him. For me my restoration was not of belief but of love. As always the restoration was followed by Christ's command of service: 'Feed my lambs, take care of my sheep, feed my sheep.'

Peter responds by drawing a line in the sand and obeys Christ's command, 'Follow me.' The Holy Spirit comes at Pentecost, Peter addresses the crowd, and on just one occasion 3,000 are saved. What a total turn around. From being cowardly to being bold – making a public proclamation about Jesus. How wonderful are the words Jesus says to him 'Upon this rock I will build my church'!

As spoken to Peter, God told me through His Word how deep his love is for me; that He is the restorer; that when I return I was to feed His sheep; that upon this rock (Christ in me) He would build His Church.

God called me to respond like Peter by forgiving myself for confessed sins I had committed as a believer, to forgive other believers and to 'forget', and to follow Him by walking in my calling. I also had to choose to draw a line in the sand and to move forward.

If you know the story of Ruth and Naomi you know that Naomi was led away from Bethlehem. Bethlehem means 'the house of bread'. Her husband took her away because there was a famine, so they actually left looking for bread. She was a prodigal who was hurting and tattered to the point that she changed her name from Naomi, meaning pleasant, to Mara meaning bitter.

The word tells us that after the deaths of her husband and sons, she returns to Bethlehem, the house of bread, with Ruth and she eats of the bread of life in all its fullness, with the fulfilment of all her dreams and desires and ambitions.

God's presence is the place of bread; Jesus is the place of bread. He is the bread of life. We, individually and as the church, need to be a safe place of bread for the hungry and for the hurting. But to do this we need to see ourselves as Jesus sees us. We are his masterpiece!

I was hungry and had been looking for bread. I had left the place of bread, looking for bread.

I had physically and emotionally disengaged from God, the church and other relationships.

Naomi had believed a lie; she believed that God had dealt bitterly with her instead of the truth that God is love. Satan kills, steals and destroys – not God.

I had believed so many lies. It was time to return to the bread of life, and I did.

When the prodigal son returned to his father, the father broke all the social rules of etiquette by lifting his robe and running to his son. God does the same to us. Whether we have been running away in the unbelief of our thoughts, words or actions, God is ready to sweep us up in his arms and feast with us and put his cloak of righteousness around us.

Yippee!

God ran towards me to embrace and love me. I was lifted in his arms knowing that:

'There is now no condemnation for those who are in Christ Jesus.' Romans 8:1.

Satan tries to paralyse the church by getting us stuck in our pasts, our mistakes, unbelief, hurt, offence, lack of forgiveness and fear, lack of knowledge and a lack of understanding of our new identity in Jesus. I woke up to the truth, which is that as a Christian, Christ is in me, with me and for me!

My eyes were opened to a sense of the 'now', and that eternal life in Jesus was not just about dying and not going to hell. It was about living, 'eternal quality living', in the present!

Yes! It was time to enjoy the journey – the journey of life. It was time to fly and enjoy the rich, limitless, endless, overflowing, abundant 'shalom' – peace – nothing broken, nothing missing, living in Jesus.

God said to me through His Word, 'Talitha cumi', meaning 'little girl, arise'. And, 'She's not dead, but asleep.' Yes, it was time to arise. I had been sleeping for so long.

When Jesus raised Lazarus from the dead in John 11:38 'He called out in a loud voice, "Lazarus, come out!"' Well – I came out, my hands and feet wrapped with strips of linen, and a cloth around my face. But I came out: by faith.

Jesus said to them, 'Take off the grave clothes and let him go.'

Others helped me to take off my grave clothes so that I could go –

and I danced,
and I sang,
and I skipped,
and I did cartwheels!

'But for you who revere my name the sun of righteousness will rise with healing in its wings. And you will go out and leap like calves released from the stall.' Malachi 4:2.

builders

'They will rebuild the ancient ruins
and restore the places long devastated;
they will renew the ruined cities
that have been devastated for generations.'

isaiah 61:4

photography: richard farquhar

reflection, revelation, restoration

Family life

There are houses and there are homes – Trish and Padraig Deeley have a wonderful home full of love, life and the noise of laughter from their four, fun-loving children.

Everything about this house says, 'Family life is great!' Splashes of feminine pinks and contrasting masculine blues are incorporated with bold blacks and an assortment of neutral shades throughout the house.

photography: barbara egan - www.reportage.ie

The long galley kitchen is as much an essential part of the house as the lounge. Velux windows allow the light to pour into this relaxed space where you can cook, chill out and put on the jukebox.

fairy lights

'I love fairy lights, and even have to have them in the kitchen,' says Trish – she has them tucked around the parsley and tin pot of garlic on her window ledge.

A mix of coloured crockery is displayed in the blue glass-fronted wall units. Solid wooden worktops and an assortment of accessories and light, soft furnishings complement the cool duck egg blue units.

'This room is where we all hang out and have fun as a family. It's a great place for the kids to play,' says Trish.

'The "sticky finger friendly," denim blue slipcovers have been washed more times than I can remember, and always look as good as new,' says Trish, who suggests that every family home should have them!

'There used to be an unusual store in Dublin called Grines & Co. It was known as the house with the red door, and was owned by an American lady, and everything was always for sale. I fell in love with a bright, floral piece of fabric stretched over a frame; it was hanging on a mantle over a fireplace. Upon enquiring about its price, I was told that it was not for sale which surprised me because everything else was. The lady had bought the fabric from a fabric show in Finland and she loved it. About to relocate back home to America, she had decided to take it with her. Every time I went into the store, I told her how much I loved it because it was so happy, bright and vibrant in colour! Thankfully three days before she returned home, she decided it was too big to take with her, and so she sold it to me,' says Trish.

It's great when we enjoy our environment, and it reflects our personalities - occupied by three boys and three girls, democracy regarding the interior design was a must for the entire household. 'I appreciate life, and love being a wife and mum', says Trish - who has had so much satisfaction in doing up the home with, and for, the family.

Padraig and Trish, who are both from Dublin, had actually met in America, thanks to a mutual friend of theirs who was visiting. Once down the aisle, and some years later, they left Boston with their then three children to attend a wedding back in their homeland of Dublin, Ireland.

For some time they had been toying with the idea of buying an investment property. After only being home for a few days, their attention was drawn to a red brick terrace property - now their home.

Padraig, who has his own building company called Deeley Construction, recognised the potential of the house immediately. Trish, with her flair for interior design, saw beyond its then dingy appearance, and could imagine the house renovated and fully decorated. The house had so many original features with its high ceilings and beautifully tiled antique fireplaces - it was bursting with character.

The sitting room is the place to relax and flick through house magazines, with your feet up on the ottoman. The room is at the front of the house, and is bright and airy, with light reflected in the large mirror over the original fireplace. What with comfortable chairs, a sofa and an open fire, on cold winter nights the sitting room is where Trish and Padraig like to snuggle up together and take time out from the business of the day.

The short trip became a six-month mission of carefully restoring the old property that was built in 1902. 'Fortunately the roof was sound enough, but if you shut the doors too hard the ceilings would fall down,' laughs Trish.

The house needed to be re-plumbed and, for investment purposes, the couple decided to put in two ensuites so that the property could be used as bed and breakfast accommodation.

With so much happening to the house, it was a good time to redesign the layout. The attic space was utilised and made into a large bedroom with an ensuite bathroom.

With the house re-wired, damp eliminated, rotting plaster replaced, new ceilings, new flooring, new plumbing and a new kitchen, the job was done and their mission was over.

Back in Boston things seemed different, and Padraig and Trish felt a stirring that Dublin was now to be their home. Six weeks later, with bags packed and a sofa and bed on the way from America, the family returned home to Dublin, Ireland - this time to stay – well, at least for now!

Dining room

The chimneybreast is painted with black chalkboard paint, highlighting the white mirror and contrasting with the vibrant pink chairs. 'I re-upholstered them myself with velvet fabric and the help of a staple gun,' says Trish laughing, and commenting that they look good if you don't look too closely!

he crockery
upboard
as a junk
hop find.
ish showed
some tender
ving
are and a
aintbrush.

So much had changed in the time they had lived abroad but having kids help them adapt quickly. Trish's main focus was on getting the children settled in schools. They were very happy and everything went smoothly. With Dublin booming, it had become a place that attracted a lot of Europeans and Americans, so the couple made lots of new friends of different nationalities.

'I like to use clothes like pieces of art', says Trish, who adds colour to her room with a summer coat, a dressmaker's dummy and shoes.

An old painted wardrobe that had its mirror replaced with chicken wire has become home to a selection of coloured, folded sheets. 'I don't iron my sheets,' exclaims Trish proudly.

'Our faith in God is very important to us and we see His hand in our lives.'

Now, some nine years later, they look back and laugh at how they were both originally from Dublin, met in America, then returned to Dublin for a wedding, and ended up moving back home. 'Our faith in God is very important to us and we see His hand in our lives,' says Trish who encourages the children in their faith.

Over the years the house has undergone a number of facelifts, and has changed in its use and style. 'With my youngest aged seven, the house is not as child-friendly as it used to be,' says Trish, who has still ensured that the home is low maintenance, and keeps the rooms looking clutter-free by having lots of baskets for easy storage.

For the Deeleys, home is about living in a place of happiness together. 'I am so blessed. Life is good and I am enjoying it. We have our faith in God, our health, each other, love and a beautiful home', says Trish who has enjoyed the journey, savouring every moment.

Cian and Killian love their room - the converted attic - and proudly display the American flag - the country where they were both born.

Emma's room is 'really girlie-pink', what with fairy lights draped around the original fireplace, and a pretty pink dolls' house. Any little girl would love this room!

artwork: dermot mcconaghy   design: www.markflint.net

reflection, revelation, restoration

At 29 I had a miscarriage and then a hysterectomy.

In my bedroom I had a grand mirror that leant against the wall, almost floor to ceiling. From standing in front of the mirror with my hands tucked under my tummy, enjoying the delight of my small bump ...

... I stood there with no baby and no womb.

I looked pregnant with the swelling, but the bruises and staples brought me quickly back to harsh reality.

I was no stranger to miscarriages, but there had always been the hope that I would conceive again – that was now a dream that I could no longer cling to.

I was living abroad at the time, and as a well-seasoned survivor I cruised along numbly through grief and an automatically kick-started menopause.

Nothing could have prepared me for my Jekyll and Hyde irrational behaviour: mood swings, hot flushes and tears that I so desperately tried to suppress.

For years I was left feeling very confused and my spiritual walk was a rollercoaster ride, based upon my emotions and 'liquidised' theologies. By that I mean blended, confused and mixed up beliefs.

I had drawn a line in the sand like one freed from the grave clothes, yet I was still living like a 'yo-yo'.

Daily striving to be stable, fighting myself and the chaos of my feelings that ruled my thoughts – it seemed like I would take one step forward and fifteen back – like one swimming in quicksand.

Then one day I had a revelation of the consistency of the Word and the love of God. His love indwelling me was my anchor and my stability – what a relief that was!

Yes, the light quite literally went on.

I was to stop basing who I was in God by what I felt or by my circumstances – rather I was to live in the truth of what the Word of God says.

I had to step back from situations and how I felt, take a deep breath and re-align my thoughts onto the Word and who I was in Jesus.

I was amazed by the results. It was like pressing a pause button on a remote control.

I could change the atmosphere rather than allowing the atmosphere to dictate to me. Walking in the Word I could be a thermostat instead of a thermometer.

Living in the Word I could be a vessel of God used to regulate moods, situations, environments and circumstances. In the Word I could have a consistent and stable walk rather than being dictated to and influenced by externals.

In the Word I was free to change, move forward and be equipped to embrace, step into and sustain stability in my calling and destiny. I had heard it said, but it was true – the truth sets us free.

After all, the Word is the same yesterday, today and forever. It certainly was my stability and my peace in a storm.

So, if I could live by the Word and who the Word says I am, I won't just react, but I would respond 'in faith'.

OK – sometimes I would take a deep breath, bite my tongue almost off, and sit down and have a cup of tea and a huge bit of chocolate cake.

But I still responded in faith.

So I asked myself, 'Where do I start?'

The answer was quick – 'In the Word.'

And so I went about writing out cards, simple but very effective. I needed all the help I could get!

There were cards everywhere: the sink, the fridge, the loo, the laundry basket ... to name a few places. Yes! You name it, there was a card. My thoughts had become such a mess that I had to get right back to basics.

Believing and living the Word caused me to walk in stability.

I needed to know who was the God that so loved me.

John 1:1 – 'In the beginning was the Word, and the Word was with God, and the Word was God. He was with God in the beginning.'

John 14:6 – 'Jesus said, "I am the way, the truth and the life."'

1 John 14:16 – 'God is love.' God is the Ancient of Days, the Alpha and Omega, the Word, the Way, Truth, Life, Love and my Saviour.

I need to know who I am to God.

John 3:16 – 'For God so loved the world, that he gave his one and only Son, that whoever believes in him shall not perish but have eternal life.'

2 Corinthians 5:17,18 – 'Therefore, if anyone is in Christ, he is a new creation, the old has gone, the new has come. All this is from God, who reconciled us to himself through Christ and gave us the ministry of reconciliation.'

Ephesians 2:10 – 'For we are God's workmanship, created in Christ Jesus to do good works, which God prepared in advance for us to do.'

I needed to know that God is for me.

Romans 8:31 – 'If God is for us, who can be against us?'

That was my reality. I had to let the words 'God is for me' resonate through my very being until I really believed it. That way I could walk in love and avoid being drawn into discord.

If I believed this truth, I would not react out of insecurity and fear of rejection or failure.

I needed to know that as a Christian I am one with Christ.

1 Corinthians 6:17 – 'But he who unites himself with the Lord is one with him in spirit.'

Such wonder, to know that as a Christian I am one with God. I had passed from darkness into light! Wow, He envelops me!

I needed to know that Christ is my stability.

Hosea 2:19,20 – 'And I will betroth you to me forever; yes I will betroth you to me in righteousness and justice in steadfast love and in mercy. I will even betroth you to me in stability and in faithfulness and you shall know, recognise, be acquainted with, appreciate give heed to, and cherish the Lord.'

I needed to listen and give attention to the Word.

Proverbs 4:20 – 'My son, give attention to my words, incline your ear to my sayings. Do not let them depart from your sight, keep them in the midst of your heart for they are life to those who find them and health to all their body.'

The Word is my daily tonic, my vitamin C, my soul food, my emotional and my physical health. It changes how I think, how I exist and how I see myself and see others.

I needed to recognise the body's true purpose. Understanding myself and my make-up helped me.

1 Corinthians 3:16 – 'Don't you know that you yourselves are God's temple and that God's Spirit lives in you.'

I realised that as a Christian my body's true purpose was to cover like a veil my new recreated spirit in the image of Jesus Christ – the glory of God, in me!

I am spirit, soul (mind, will and emotions) and flesh. To be in control of myself, I had to understand that the flesh's senses and emotions are dead, and that they have nothing to do with the spirit of who I am in Jesus. I am reborn and recreated in Jesus!

Jesus Christ – the Word who indwells me and is one with me – controls my thermostat.

In my snug I have a funky retro old radio. It doesn't tune in very well and just makes a terrible noise, but it looks great! Instead of having it rewired, I have hidden on the inside of it another new radio that I use to tune into the right station.

While giving it a dust, it dawned on me that my physical make-up is like the radio. My flesh without the Word doesn't tune in well, but my recreated spirit – joined with God on the inside – is always in tune like the new radio and always perfect.

The old radio is like my flesh that is often on the wrong wavelength, but the new radio is the 'I am', 'the Word' in me. Christ in me is reliable and trustworthy!

Galatians 2:20 – 'I have been crucified with Christ and I no longer live, but Christ lives in me. The life I now live in the body, I live by faith in the Son of God, who loved me and gave himself for me.'

I no longer live but Christ lives in me. I needed to bring my carnal mind into alignment with the mind of Christ, through the renewing of my mind with the Word.

I needed to take authority over the flesh.

Genesis 25:33,34 – Esau sold his birthright for bread, stew and lentils because he was hungry. Esau made a bad life-changing decision based upon what his flesh dictated to him. I need to not listen to the dictates of my flesh.

Corinthians 6:12,13 – 'All things are lawful unto me, but I will not be brought under power of any. Meats for the belly, and the belly for meat.'

'OK, girl, you can do it – its time to take authority over yourself' I said with a willingness to change and gritted teeth.

I needed to rise above emotions that lied to me.

2 Timothy 1:7 – 'For God did not give us a spirit of timidity (of cowardice, of craven and cringing and fawning fear) but [He has given us a spirit] of power and of love and of a calm and well-balanced mind and discipline and self-control.'

Isaiah 41:10 – 'Fear not for I am with you, be not dismayed, for I am your God. I will strengthen you, yes, I will help you, I will uphold you with My righteous right hand.'

My stability in God brought about self-control and a continuity of love regardless of my circumstances and my emotions.

I needed to live love.

1 Corinthians 13:1 – 'And now I will show you the most excellent way. If I speak in the tongues of men and of angels, but have not love, I am only a resounding gong or a clanging cymbal. If I have the gift of prophecy and can fathom all the mysteries and all knowledge, and if I have the faith that can move mountains, but have not love, I am nothing. If I give all I possess to the poor and surrender my body to the flames, but have not love, I gain nothing. Love is patient, love is kind, it does not envy, it does not boast, it is not proud. It is not rude, it is not self-seeking, it is not easily angered, it keeps no record of wrongs. Love does not delight in evil but rejoices with truth. It always protects, always trusts, always hopes, always perseveres. Love never fails.'

In Jesus I am love and can 'choose' to display His love. His love indwells me even if I don't feel it.

1 John 4:17 – 'Dear friends, let us love one another, for love comes from God. Everyone who loves has been born of God and knows God.'

I needed to be fully persuaded of the love of God for me and for His people. I need to love myself as Jesus loves me.

Knowing and living love causes me to function in the 'shalom' – in the nothing missing, nothing broken, wholeness and peace of God, and produces the fruit of no insecurities and no hidden agendas.

Romans 8:38 – 'For I am persuaded beyond doubt (am sure) that neither death nor life, nor angels, nor principalities, nor things impending and threatening, nor things to come, nor powers, nor height, nor depth, nor anything else in all creation will be able to separate us from the love of God which is in Christ Jesus our Lord.'

I needed to be FULLY PERSUADED about my identity in Christ. God is love and He indwells me, I am His love made manifest.

1 John 14:16,18 – 'And so we know and rely on the love God has for us. There is no fear in love. But perfect love drives out fear, because fear has to do with punishment.' God wanted me to see myself as He saw me – this is His true worship and was how I could fully love Him.

I needed to guard my thoughts.

Isaiah 26:3 – 'You will guard him and keep him in perfect and constant peace whose mind (both its inclination and its character) is stayed on you because he commits himself to you, leans on you and hopes confidently in you.' So trust in the Lord.

Satan could do nothing about my position in Christ, but he could deceive my mind if I allow him to, by suggesting to me a twisted and distorted image of who God is and who I am in Christ.

Philippians 4:8 – 'Finally, brethren, whatsoever things are true, whatsoever things are honest, whatsoever things are lovely, whatsoever things are of good report, if there be any virtue and if there be any praise, think on these things.'

I had to stop thinking about lemons for my mouth to stop tasting bitter. I had been thinking about all the wrong things – you know – fear, anxiety, what people think about me – the typical kind of stuff. I needed to cast down imaginations.

2 Corinthians 10:5 – 'We demolish arguments and every pretension that sets itself up against the knowledge of God, and we take captive every thought to make it obedient to Christ.'

God said to me through His Word 'Do not go any further down the road of anything not of His highest love, highest praise, highest joy – stop! It's not of Me; it's not my spiritual blessing.' I need to guard myself from forming mental pictures and schemes opposed to God.

I needed to stop comparing myself to others.

Peter straight away after his restoration wanted to know what was going to happen to John. Jesus answers in John 21:22 – 'If I want him to remain alive until I return, what is that to you? You must follow me.' Jesus told him to focus on his own walk.

So many times I had been distracted by an unhealthy interest in the affairs of others. For me, comparing myself to others was like throwing manure on weeds. It cultivated insecurities and fears, causing me to be critical of others and of myself, normally resulting in pride, oversensitivity or control.

I needed to stop fault finding.

Matthew 7:3 – 'And why do you look at the speck in your brother's eye, but do not consider the plank in your own eye?'

My relationships blossomed and changed when I stopped trying to fix everyone else but focused on my walk with God and being His love vessel. Numbers 12:1 – Miriam and Aaron began to talk against Moses. It says that the Lord heard this, and in Numbers 12:8 said, 'Why then were you not afraid to criticize him?'

I needed to stop grumbling.

Philippians 2:14 – I will do all things without grumbling and fault finding and complaining (against God) and questioning and doubting.

I had to choose to change my thinking and stop meditating on thoughts that damage me, like grumbling, which always made me turn in on myself and caused fear, anxiety and unbelief. Instead I had to choose to think about the Word of God and good things. Obviously my thoughts created a by-product of my reaction and my response to life and all its colour.

I needed to create new memories, and re-program my thinking in line with the Word of God.

Proverbs 7:1 - 'My son, keep my words; lay up within you my commandments [for use when needed] and treasure them.'

My reactions needed to stop being based on past experiences, emotions and fears. I often had preconceived ideas and pre-judged conversations and other people's intent, based on previous memories. The best example of this was when I remarried: for sometime I would presume what Samuel was going to say or do based upon the past eight years of interaction with my previous partner.

I had to stop jumping to conclusions.

I needed to guard my heart.

When I drive a car the vehicle is a mode of transportation to get me around. I choose whom or what I let into the vehicle. The doors are like the gatekeeper of my heart. I can choose what I let in the car and what I let out. In the same way I can choose what thoughts I allow in and meditate on. Words over me only have the power I give them.

Proverbs 4:23 - 'Above all else, guard your heart, for it is the wellspring of life.'

I had to get rid of some unwanted passengers I had been carrying in my heart - some of which were hurt, offence, bitterness, self-hatred, pride and fear. I also had to harden not my heart but my mind by not allowing anything of darkness in.

I needed to talk nice to me.

For me, one of my biggest challenges was talking nice to me!

I had to start to speak faith over myself.

Proverbs 23:7 - 'For as he thinketh in his heart, so is he.'

I found that I would speak faith publicly, but internally have a conversation of unbelief. I was the voice of accusation within. Justifying my unbelief was expressing a denial of Christ, my hope of glory.

I needed to encourage myself.

Psalm 42:11 - 'Why are you in despair my soul? Why are you disturbed within me? Hope in God! For I shall praise him, the saving help of my countenance, and my God.'

I had to stop throwing myself pity parties and instead discipline my mind and confession.

I found great encouragement when I read that King David, the man after

God's own heart encouraged himself. So I decided that instead of doing my normal blurting out all the 'woe is me' stuff to any listening ear, I would take a leaf out of David's book.

I would speak the Word over myself and remember the faithfulness of God. 'You are a called, anointed, blessed daughter of the Most High, walking in God's favour'. Standing on the promises of God causes me to fly.

I needed to confess faith.

My confession had to be a confession of stability in line with the Word of God. My confession could be consistent, even if my emotions were not. My confession was my confidence in God and His promises.

Hebrews 10:35 – 'Do not fling away your fearless confidence, for it carries a great and glorious compensation of reward.'

I needed to endure by remaining standing.

Ephesians 6:13 – 'Therefore take up the whole armour of God, that you may be able to withstand in the evil day, and having done all, to stand.'

I had to stand upon the Word of truth until it grew in me and a physical change took place. I became fully aware that I exercise my mind to an opinion and was producing fruit of the opinion. I was the product of what I was thinking. I had to choose to stand by faith on the promises of God rather than how my circumstance made me feel. I had a choice – what I believed, what I meditate on and how I reacted.

I needed to trust in God.

Psalm 57:2 – 'I will cry to God Most High, who performs on my behalf and rewards me [who brings to pass His purposes for me and surely completes them]'!

God is our solution and He performs. Living in the reality of this revelation is His worship.

I needed to grow in the atmosphere of my confession of the Word of God. God was telling me to not even entertain the thought of anxious distractions. He performs on my behalf and He is my solution. I had to live in the reality of this wonderful revelation.

I needed to live in prayer, thanksgiving and peace.

Philippians 4:6,7 – 'Do not be anxious about anything but in everything by prayer and petition, with thanksgiving, present your requests to God. And the peace of God, which transcends all understanding, will guard your hearts and minds in Christ Jesus.'

My rolling everything onto Jesus was my peace. An apparent crisis could not rob me of peace unless I allowed it to.

I needed to continue to press on forgetting what was behind.

Philippians 3:13 – 'But one thing I do; forgetting what is behind and straining towards what is ahead, I press on towards the goal to win the prize to which God has called me heavenwards in Christ Jesus.'

I realised that looking back for me was a huge heart issue of unbelief – it was like I was saying to God, 'Must I bid goodbye?'

God had taken me by the hand and led me away from destruction like the angels took Lot's wife by the hand and led her out of Sodom and Gomorrah. She loitered as she looked back, and was caught up in the destruction. Every time I looked back I slipped into the fallout of old sin, unbelief and poor me.

All the time I was looking back I was being double minded about 'the now' and 'the future'.

I found that others tried to make me look back, and I had to be strong and say that I was not going there even in conversation. (Now, the only time I allow myself to look back is at the faithfulness of God, and that is to encourage myself.)

I needed to walk in my inheritance.

Romans 8:15 – 'For you did not receive a spirit that makes you a slave again to fear, but you received a spirit of sonship. And by him we cry, "Abba Father".'

I had to walk in the reality of my inheritance as a queen, princess and daughter of the King of Kings. The 'I Am' in me was my permanent state of fullness.

Psalm 23 – 'The Lord is my shepherd I shall not want.'

In Jesus my cup overflows.

I needed to know my authority in Jesus.

Colossians 2:9,10 – 'For in Christ all the fullness of the Deity lives in bodily form, and you have been given fullness in Christ, who is the head over every power and authority.'

As a Christian, the all-powerful, all mighty, ruler over every angelic principality and power indwelt me. So I had to stop praying words of unbelief and living in a defeatist attitude.

When I walk into a room Christ walks into it, in me and with me. I had to let the revelation of the finished work of Calvary be dominant in my hearing, heart, thinking, behaviour and speech.

I needed to be still.

Psalm 46:10 – 'Be still and know that I am God.'

I needed to spend quality time with God in prayer and in His Word, listening to the voice of the Holy Spirit. More and more I was aware that, even in a noisy environment, I could practice stillness in God.

I needed to know I had a purpose.

Jeremiah 29:11 – 'For I know the plans I have for you declares the Lord, plans to prosper you and not to harm you, plans to give you a hope and a future.'

My hope was in God's destiny for me and His plan for my life. God always caused me to prosper, walking in such favour and fullness of hopes, dreams and potential in Him.

I love the story in Mark 4:35 when Jesus calms the storm.

It's always warmed my heart, especially the bit when it says that the disciples were afraid (probably freaking out) and Jesus was sleeping with His head on a pillow!

Jesus had already told them that they were going to the other side.

He has said the same to His children; so in faith when the storms rage and the boat is flooding with water, we can remain rational and stable as we place our confidence in Him and put our head with His on the pillow.

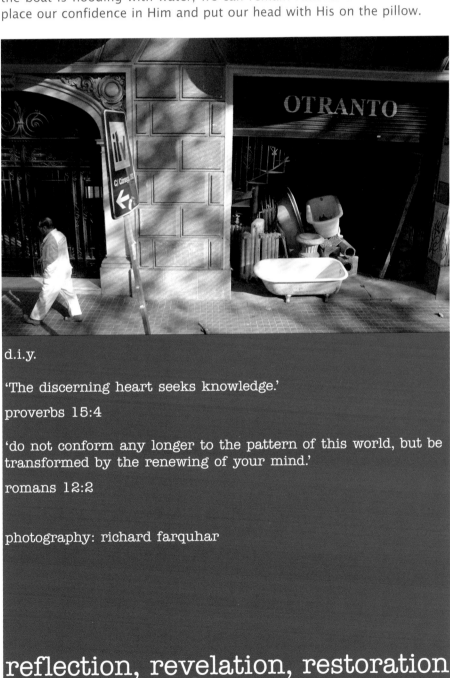

d.i.y.

'The discerning heart seeks knowledge.'
proverbs 15:4

'do not conform any longer to the pattern of this world, but be transformed by the renewing of your mind.'
romans 12:2

photography: richard farquhar

reflection, revelation, restoration

When searching for his bachelor pad, the words 'location, location, location' were at the forefront of Tom Smyth's mind. His determination not to settle for anything but the best paid off when he learned of a seafront apartment with high ceilings and an open-plan living space that was about to be built. Best of all, it was just 20 minutes from Belfast so, without hesitation Tom signed along the dotted line and agreed to the strict one-year construction and completion date.

Very soon, however, he met Elaine and, just as the apartment was finished, the two got married, putting paid to his bachelor-pad ideas! 'Whenever we were having our debates about decorating the apartment,' recalls Elaine, 'Tom would refer to Frank Lopez's apartment in the movie Scarface. In the end I watched the film to see what all the fuss was about and I had to agree: the apartment was amazing. So I hate to admit it, but the inspiration for our décor came from a gangster film!'

As soon as the newlyweds moved into their new home, they decided to hire a van and pay a visit to Ikea. Elaine still remembers having to make six trips to the van as they got carried away with the excitement of their purchases. 'There wasn't too much logic to what we picked up: we just bought what we liked on impulse. I can't really believe how well it all goes together,' she says, laughing.

'It feels like we are living on a boat!'

A huge leather corner sofa from MFI is a favourite place to relax in the open plan living space.

en Tom Smyth set out to buy a bachelor pad in Belfast, getting the right location was key.
w the contemporary interior is equally perfect for him and his new wife, Elaine.

The couple's minimalist
approach is far from cold
and stark: in fact, it's
incredibly inviting.
'Not only does the glass-
doored veranda allow light
and the sound of waves to
pour in, we also get the
breathtaking view of passing
sea cruisers, making it a kind
of exotic hideaway for us,'
explains Elaine.

To add to this atmosphere, the couple have carefully thought about where to place their furniture. A large corner sofa takes centre stage in the living area, while a lime- green cushion and vibrant hand-made alternatives add warmth and texture to the leather. 'I fell in love with the leather rug,' says Elaine. 'The dark green and brown strips remind me of seaweed, and it feels great under my feet when I'm sitting down, watching a movie. It was an inspired buy as, although the floor tiles underneath are easy to keep clean, they can feel quite cold and I'm not a huge fan of slippers,' she explains.

One of the things the couple most love about their home is the way each area flows into the next, making the whole space incredibly easy to live in. When it came to choosing her brand-new kitchen, Elaine opted for a walnut design, as the rich colour and the simplicity of the lines complemented the adjoining dining area. Despite buying the table from Habitat more than six years ago, Tom thinks it sits well in his new home. 'It's a timeless piece – in fact, I think they still sell it,' he says.

Wanting a striking look for their kitchen, the couple settled on dark walnut units.

The scheme is softened by white walls and well chosen accessories.

A separate study for privacy was a must for this busy couple, and Tom decided on a row of internal windows to maintain the feeling of openness. Refreshing green walls are a colourful backdrop to the comfy leather sofa and practical office furniture. 'It's actually become quite a feature,' admits Elaine. 'When you're in the living room, your eye is immediately drawn to the vibrant wall colour.'

The master bedroom is a honeymooner's dream, with a fantastic ensuite, plasma television and an over-the-top table for weekend breakfasts. 'It's a fabulous room to wake up in,' enthuses Elaine. 'You can relax in bed while looking out to sea - it makes you feel as if you're on a boat!' The colour theme for the room was inspired by a beautiful oil painting hung over the bed. 'I wasn't sure if such a bold wall colour would work in here, but I think it makes the room feel cosy and inviting,' she adds.

The unusual low-level window is one of the couple's favourite features, allowing them to enjoy the sea view from their bed.

Both of the guest bedrooms have been given an individual look with striking colours and sumptuous accessories.

'Our first 2 years of marriage feel as if they have been spent in a luxury honeymoon suite,' confesses Elaine. 'We have to keep pinching ourselves to remind us this is actually our home!'

Using a large dinner plate as a stencil, Elaine cleverly jazzed up the plain white walls with some leftover red paint.

With its dark wood vanity unit and sleek fittings, the main bathroom has a classic, uncluttered feel.

When it came to choosing the bathroom fittings, the couple treated themselves to a Jacuzzi bath from MFI. When investing in a new bath think carefully about the position of your taps: side-mounted ones are more flexible and will ensure a comfortable soak!

The couple couldn't fail to be impressed by the balcony and its impressive views.

Over 8 million people have now attended the Alpha Course
and had an opportunity to explore the meaning of life.
Tom and Elaine are enjoying meeting with a group
in a local church near Belfast, Northern Ireland.
'My mate has just become a Christian and he told us
about the group. We thought we would check it
out. So far it's been great, they have been
able to help clarify things and answer my
bombardment of questions' says Tom.

www.alpha.org

THEN
LOVE
PIERCED
MY
STONE
HEART
MELTED

Ezekiel 36:26 'I will give you a new heart and put a new spirit in you;

NOW

KNOWING

JESUS

LOVE

FORGIVENESS

WHOLENESS

PEACE

I will remove from you your heart of stone and give you a heart of flesh.'

As my husband Sam and I drove over the cattle grid, past the steamed up kitchen window, our bright red van caught the eye of Yvonne who came running out through the front door, clutching baby Aiden, to greet us.

With a big kiss on the cheek I was welcomed, followed by "Alright sweetie? Fancy a cuppa?" My dear, close friend was a lady after my own heart. "Fabulous, fabulous" echoed through the house, and we were soon joined by Grady, followed by Liam, Rory and Maisie.

They all looked so smart with their colour-co-ordinated outfits and new haircuts ready for the cameras. Most kids run a mile when Mum comes wielding a large pair of scissors and a bowl, but not in this house. It's always designer haircuts; with years of experience as an art director for Tony and Guy under Yvonne's belt - style is never a problem.

The mood was one of excitement. "My tummy is rumbling," said Sam, clutching an overnight bag and goodies under his arm. With that, Steve the photographer arrived. We knew that after all the hard work, we would get to join in a delicious meal. Our mutt Indie took the lead into the house, and made herself comfortable on the sofa; this was her second home.

Before long Grady and Yvonne were scurrying around in the kitchen, knocking up some fantastic, tongue-tantalising delight. It's never a rich tea biscuit or a custard cream in this house. Grady owned a restaurant called 'The Dream Café' in the USA. I suppose knocking up a quick blackberry crumble and café latte was "no problemo" to him, although I am never quite sure who is the best cook, as Yvonne always rustles us up gourmet delights, and she was the chef in charge of the feast.

The very arty coat rack that one of them had obviously constructed out of an old piece of distressed wood and some pretty hooks distracted me. What caught my eye was not the deep warm green, although the richness of the colour was quite impressive. No, it was the hat. I found myself reminiscing, off in my own little dream world.

The words of a song started to spring up into my mind. "Wherever I lay my hat; that's my home." As a child, I remember long journeys in the car with my Mum and Dad's worn-out selection of old tapes and a tin of boiled sweets coated in icing sugar. I used to put my fingers in my ears, desperately trying to drown out yet another tune from Dire Straits, the Carpenters or Neil Diamond that played time and time again.

My time warp was shattered as a latte was thrust into my hand. "Awful hat, isn't it? He insists on hanging it there; doesn't go with the coats at all," proclaimed Yvonne in disbelief! As a stylist, I could take her point. She knew I would be a sympathetic ear! "Oh, Yvonne! I love my hat. It keeps my ears warm. Hey babes! I love you, you're so cute." Egged on by Sam, Grady laughed as he winked at me, teasing her.

Nana's professional knitting skill is passed on to three generations. Yvonne follows Mum's footsteps, ensuring that all the kids can knit.

The blanket box made by Grady doubles up as a coffee table.

Grady and Yvonne smiled at each other as I admired the funky coat with green fur and turquoise check, decoratively hanging like a piece of art. I had one of those deep and meaningful moments, thinking to myself how relevant the words of the song were in their lives, when a light turned on in my memory. That was it! Name that tune in one: Paul Young. Grady had laid down his hat, and he and the family were home.

The thought provoked a question. "Where is home?" I asked Yvonne. She was originally from Southern Ireland, and had spent years in America, including in Dallas, Texas, where she met Grady, led him to the Lord, and married him. Grady's ancestors were from Ireland, and as a single man, he had visited Northern Ireland.

"God is our home"

I followed her into the kitchen for some girlie time, whilst the guys took themselves off to the garden outhouse. I said again,"Where is home, Yvonne?" "Home is a place called 'there'," she said; her eyes were filled with joyous tears.

As a couple, they had followed Jesus everywhere He had sent them. They were international globetrotters. Umm, I thought as I digested her words "home is a place called 'there'," I got it; God was their home, anchor and fixed heavenly abode.

She shared with me how God had led them to this beautiful, quaint 100-year-old farmhouse in Broughshane. When viewing the property for rent, the agent pointed out that there was a raven's nest by the house, and warned them of the noise. For Yvonne, this was a reminder of the promise of God for His provision, as she thought about how Elijah was fed by the ravens.

Hey, nice coffee machine! That's new. "Yes - it's Grady's gift from Jesus. Grady saw the machine in a rather swanky shop, and thought to himself how much he would like it. A few days later, it arrived at the house as a gift," she said with a smile of utter delight.

The family scripture is written on the stark blackboard with white chalk. John 10:10 'I have come that they may have life.'

It looked great in the 'French feel' kitchen that I had given a face-lift, spending only £40. The contents of four tester pots colour-washed the walls. Tile paint transformed the white tiles, the vigorous use of a razor and pan scourers on them provided a distressed finish, exposing some of the old patterned tiles. Tea towel fabric on wooden dowels fills in where the original doors were missing, and the old strip lighting was covered by chicken mesh for a softer look to the room. The bare face of an old refrigerator was disguised and jazzed up by a piece of plywood covered in blackboard paint.

"Thank you Daddy, for blessing the food..."

Grace

The day passed by so fast; there was so much to talk about, so much to catch up on. Life for the O'Briens was full, what with the opening and running of Charis Bible College, the family's feet had hardly touched the ground.

www.cbcireland.org

A photograph of him at the Giant's Causeway hangs proudly on their bedroom wall. Whilst in Ireland for their honeymoon, he just fell in love with the place.

A wrought iron, wall-mounted garden pot stand creates a beautiful headboard.

With anticipation I stood by, wearing my elasticated skirt and loose top to ensure enough room for all the grub. My heart was moved as I saw the love of Jesus made manifest in this family and their lives as they gave thanks. It was time to praise God for His faithfulness, provision, direction, love, grace and tender mercies. It was time to tuck in!

The room was filled with talk of all that God had done: how He led them from being graduates of Charis Bible College, America and England, to establish a new work in County Antrim.

Matthew 4:19
"Come, follow me," Jesus said, " and I will make you fishers of men."
With students dedicated to learning and spreading the good news, we celebrated Jesus, our good news. As I left the next day, I smiled reading the hand written plaque over the door: 'You are about to enter the mission field.'

individuality

"Everything that is really great and inspiring is created by the individual who can labor in freedom"

TIME	ADDRESS	MODE	RESU
	17123 9810		OK
	9 984		
17:11	171 43 5728	TE	OK
9:49	917 8 0		
13:07			
13:51			
14:		TESM	
14:50	91755555 73486132	TESM	

TIME:	ADDRESS	MODE
13:04		RS
14:01	019 15113	RS

An 'off the record' chat about styling like the magazines style.

In most homes the hub of the house is the kitchen. It is the room where there is food, fun and laughter around the fridge. From toast in the morning with the kids to preparing a candlelit dinner - the kitchen is a place of life and energy.

Eye-catching packaging is great to use when accessorising a kitchen. Our supermarket shelves are bunged with food packaged so artistically that a kitchen can be decked out like an edible gallery.

Coloured glass bottles of water, herbal teas, tinned filter coffee, fancy crisps, crusty loaves, homemade jam, jars with pulses, dried fruit or pasta, dishes with fruit or vegetables, pots of herbs, cookery books, coffee pots, breadboards and so the list goes on – all these can be used to add vitality and decorate the kitchen space.

In our zeal we can over do it: often less is more - a dish with 4 pears or a few cherries will have a more dramatic impact than a mixed bowl of fruit. Getting the balance is the thing; you don't want clutter, but, on the other hand, you don't want the room to look sterile and uninviting.

I love flowers and, in my eyes, they are a must in any house - from large flamboyant arrangements, dramatic vases, to a simple flower in a bottle or a hand-full of flowers fresh from the garden in a jam jar. My husband sometimes comes home from the forest with a bunch of pretty wild flowers. To some they are weeds, but to me they are utter beauty!

I recently returned home from a preaching engagement in England. Samuel my husband took me by the hand into our lounge and there it was – you couldn't miss it - a 32" big black screen. After 10 years without a television, I had to practice all that I had preached, believe me! If you want your home to look like the magazines, don't make the television the focal point of the lounge - even if there's football on!

A bare coffee table can be transformed with a stack of books, a small vase of flowers and a candle, dish or ornament. Plump, placed cushions make a sofa look all the more inviting. I love to snuggle up with a throw on my lap in the evenings, and think they look great draped over the arm of a sofa.

The dining room can be overspill for storage from the kitchen. Glass-fronted cupboards are both stylish and wonderful for displaying and storing all the 'special' crockery. Table-cloths, glasses, decanters and cutlery can be used just like ornaments.

For bedrooms the bedding is vital – does your bed look cosy and comfortable? We spend so much time sleeping, yet very often neglect this space. A lamp and a book at the side of the bed with a glass of water makes the room look lived in. To give a feminine touch, place fresh flowers, a few perfume bottles or jewellery on the mantlepiece or unit. A chair in the room always acts as a good accessory and says 'I come to this private space to escape and think.' I must confess I don't personally iron my sheets! For that magazine style, bedding should be crisp-looking.

Children's rooms these days seem to have so much stuff, often leaving the rooms looking small and cluttered. With so many funky storage solutions on the market, play areas can be fun, organised, stylish and easily accessible.

Fresh clean towels are a must in the bathroom, and have no half-squeezed toothpaste tubes and empty toiletry bottles on view – hide them away in a cupboard. White towels are great for simplicity, but coloured towels always lift a room. Artistically placed perfume bottles, toiletries and soaps are great to add colour and show that the bathroom is a personal spa. Unusual shells, candles and dishes can be used to give that magazine finishing touch. If you don't have an eye for colour, try to steer clear of coloured toilet rolls and use white - the blue might be on special but it could clash with the walls!

photography: richard farquhar

An office lamp, a stack of paper, dish of pencils and some glasses say 'this space is allocated to work. It's quiet and I concentrate here.' So many people work from home now and office furniture is becoming more of a fashion statement. Huge old computers and printers are a big 'no-no', but don't be quite so keen to throw out that old filing cabinet or desk. Why not mix the new with the old?

So - we all love house magazines, but, in reality, do we really want them to be 'real homes?'

NO

In my office by the end of the day my waste paper bin is overflowing, and my desk normally has an assortment of half-empty mugs of tea and tell-tale biscuit crumbs. Well, that's the reality, - and that's not mentioning the coats hanging at the bottom of the stairs, the pile of books I keep meaning to put away, the mound of ironing still in the basket and, of course, the ungroomed dog!

We like to dream - the people lifestyle shots that draw us into the picture and cause us to feel a sense of connection and involvement - the happy couple enjoying a little nibble of cake, or maybe some kids having a go at baking in the kitchen.

Wow! How desirable to just sit with our feet up and relax in that lounge! I want one - to the delight of the advertisers! I want the stunning furnishings, the newspaper or magazine and a tray of fresh coffee and that naughty pastry. Ah! How the other half live!

Oh! My taste buds are going at the thought of the meal in the dining room - a stack of white, bone china plates, the tall coloured crystal glasses, a decanter, polished cutlery, crisp linen and fresh flowers. Romance, dinner, va-va-voom!

So when we turn the pages of a house magazine or this **bookazine** - let's enjoy what we see but remember, in reality, these homes, just like our homes, sometimes have an un-made bed, a vase with half- dead roses and stagnant water, or a mouldy pear in the fruit bowl.

We all know that they like everything else could be added to the list of re-touching, along with the worn carpet and ripped wallpaper. Hey! Maybe the graphics man could even make me look two sizes slimmer! Don't get me started on that one – "another article, another time, another coffee!"

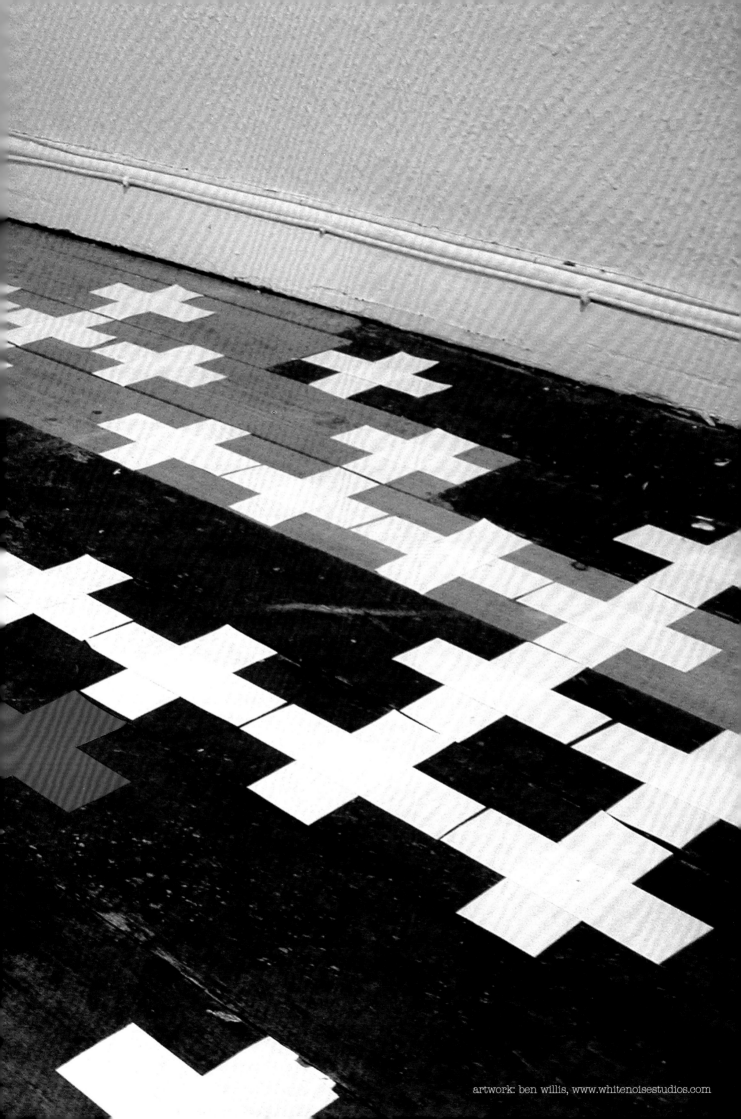

artwork: dermot mcconaghy

design: www.markflint.net

reflection, revelation, restoration

Ever since the hysterectomy, later failed marriage and period as a prodigal on the run – it felt like all my dreams had been crushed and I was left questioning my sense of purpose.

After everything that had transpired I was left feeling like a rag doll torn into shreds by a pack of wild dogs.

I read a very disturbing story in the Bible – it sent shudders down my spine. The account is in 2 Samuel 13:12. It's about a young girl called Tamar who had worn a richly ornamented robe as a sign of her royalty, her virginity and her future. In a short moment she had all her dreams snatched from her when her brother, one whom she had served and trusted, violated her. She was then thrown out onto the streets, rejected and despised by him.

I could relate to her in so many ways, as can others who have been rejected, raped – physically or emotionally – and had their dreams, their desires, their hopes, and their ambitions stolen.

As I sat on the beach some five years later, my eyes were opened and hope entered my life again – actually hope had not left me, but I had left hope.

The darkness lifted and there was a new morning and new mercies, as the sun rose across the glass-like sea.

Psalm 139:13 – 'My frame was not hidden from you when I was made in the secret place. When I was woven together in the depths of the earth, your eyes saw my unformed body. All the days ordained for me were written in your book before one of them came to be.'

Could it be – could it really be?

Even in the womb God had a destiny for my life, a plan and purpose for me?

He still knew the depths of me, my dreams, my desires and my hopes – after all, He had formed my inward parts. So if all the days ordained for me were written in His book before one of them came to pass, all this, all this mess and well-buried dreams, were no surprise to God.

I had been sad, very sad and joyless, for a long time, but now I could get up and smile again.

It was time for the butterfly to emerge and fly.

I had been given the opportunity to leave my past, bondage and unbelief and walk in the fullness of all that God had for me. In Exodus 14:10-16 I read about the Israelites who had left the bondage of Egypt to enter the Promised Land.

Very quickly when the rubber hit the road, they slipped into unbelief, looked back, turned on themselves, questioned God and turned against their leader. That sounded very familiar.

Moses answered the people:

Exodus 14:13 – 'Do not be afraid. Stand firm and you will see the deliverance the Lord will bring you today.' Exodus 14:14 – 'The Lord will fight for you; you need only to be still.' Exodus 14:15 – 'Then the Lord said to Moses, "Why are you crying out to me? Tell the Israelites to move on."'

So I had to choose not to look back and be afraid, but to stand firm in the fresh revelation I had and to move on!

So how could I move on and into what?

I found my answer in the book of Nehemiah 2:2-5. Nehemiah knew his purpose, and he had a dream to rebuild the walls of Jerusalem. The King asked Nehemiah why his face was sad. Afraid he told him why.

Like Nehemiah I had a dream, a desire and sadness inside of me. Nehemiah was sad because of the condition of the walls of Jerusalem and the need for their restoration.

I was sad because the plans and purposes God had planted in me were buried so deep – ever so deep – yet not snuffed out.

The Word was planted in him; the word was planted in me. Again the Word gave me hope. It says in Ephesians 2:10 'For we are God's workmanship, created in Christ Jesus to do good works, which God prepared in advance for us to do.'

Yes! If I wanted to live in the fullness of life with all its dreams and desires, I had to live in Christ – He had prepared in advance good works for me to do.

God had prepared in advance for Nehemiah to rebuild the walls of Jerusalem, and God gave him the opportunity and divine connection to facilitate their fulfilment.

When Nehemiah was asked why he was so sad by the king – although afraid – he told him. I thought to myself that if Nehemiah could go to the King, then so could I – so I went to the King of Kings and I told him why my face was so sad.

Grief and unbelief had caused me to shut down – first the loss of my baby, then my womb, then my husband. A wall of ice kept me safe from vulnerability, or so I thought.

Afraid like Nehemiah, I spoke; questions, answers and thoughts flowed like a pent-up flood from the very depths of my being and my heart thawed, melting before my King. A hit and miss jumble of random 'what ifs' and 'hows' and possibilities like a torrent escaped the box of dreams that had been locked up and hidden for so long.

What was my divine purpose and how could I fulfil it? How could I make a difference? Could I delight in God and expect him to accomplish His purposes through me? How could I bless others? What was I naturally gifted in? What did I enjoy and what flowed easily in my life? Had I tapped into God-given talents that He had planted in me? What were the passions that stirred me? Had I given them to God? What desires, dreams and vision could I not get out of my mind? What was producing good fruit in my life? Were my dreams, desires and vision bigger than me? What was the inner witness of the Holy Spirit saying to me? What did other mature Christians around me see in me? What did I have peace in? Was I trusting in God's ability to work through me?

As I thought about these things I was really aware that Satan had tried to delay me, or even take me out. In Exodus 2:1-9 it talks about how Moses had a destiny and that Satan tried to take his life. When he was born, Pharaoh ordered a massacre of all baby boys. Seeing that he was beautiful his mother disobeyed the command and hid him for three months, and then laid him in a basket in a river, trusting God for his life.

He was found by Pharaoh's daughter who took him in as her own. Unaware of who she was, she employed Moses' mother to raise him in the palace. Ironically, Pharaoh, the man who had tried to kill Moses as a baby, financed him having the very best of everything.

Satan had tried to take me out and I had almost allowed him to do so through my unbelief. When he had failed at that, he then tried to abort my dreams, desires and vision.

Recently there have been times when I have kept my vision hidden for its safety and even laid it down for a season to serve another's vision. Like Moses' mother who hid Moses for three months, I now knew that I would see a safe birthing and fulfilment of the Word in me – as my King made a way.

Moses knew that God had a plan for his life, and he had a desire to be used to free God's people from slavery. I read in Exodus 2:11 that one day, after Moses had grown up, he went out to where his own people were and watched them at their hard labour. He saw an Egyptian beating a Hebrew, one of his own people. Glancing this way and that, and seeing no one, he killed the Egyptian. Later, news of this got to Pharaoh and he again tried to kill Moses, so Moses ran and hid.

For a long time I had the heart of a runaway.

I had run and hidden – afraid. Afraid of what? For years I wanted to run and hide from my past, but wherever I went all my baggage went with me! Moses ran, but God had his hand on his life, and he ran into the carefully woven fibres of a rich and beautiful tapestry of his destiny in God.

Like a headless chicken I ran around in circles.

I am always multi-tasking and life can be so busy. God really spoke to me through

Exodus 3:2,3. It talks about how Moses notices a burning bush that did not burn up. He said, 'I will go over and see this strange sight.' There he met with the Lord.

I needed to take the time to enquire and to stop being so driven and hasty. I would pray, 'Lord show me your will and way', yet I would rush through, or even past, those 'moments' that could have seemed so insignificant – like a burning bush.

I was hurting, and for years I had killed time, just wishing the days away.

I asked myself the question: was it too late for me to step into my destiny and see the fulfilment of my dreams?

Then I thought about Abraham:

Hebrews 11:8 – 'By faith Abraham, when called to go to a place he would later receive as an inheritance, obeyed and went, even though he did not know where he was going.'

Well, if at the age of 75 he headed for the Promised Land – while we have breath, it is not too late. Praise God it was not too late for me!

The voice of God spoke to me one day: so still and quiet and in a crowded, noisy room. I had walked away from a situation that had left me feeling like I wanted to hide in the toilets. The voice comforted me and made me laugh. Oh how I laughed!

Without giving too much away, I will tell more. Samuel and I both had a word from God to travel abroad to minister. It was our third trip that year and we were living by faith. For some time God had been laying on our hearts that we would be start-ing a church. To date we had ministered alongside pastors. At the end of our preaching ministry trip we went to a large convention, excited about being refreshed and able to glean from the experience of other ministers before we returned home to Northern Ireland.

When we went to sign in, we were asked if we were in ministry. To which we said 'Yes'. We said that we were preachers, but believed that God was calling us to start a church one day.

The lady behind the counter would not let us register with everyone else, and insisted that we went to the 'Pastor's booth'.

My heart was pounding.

It seemed almost presumptuous of us – yet to be honest, I was also excited. I so wanted to learn from the others. The wheels had been in motion for some time – it was like we were stepping out to our destiny – we had never publicly said we felt called to start a church before.

We had our best gear on, but after living out of a suitcase for so long, we looked like ragamuffins.

(Samuel will not agree with that comment about him.)

Anyway, in front of everyone we were asked for our cards, and, upon telling the lady we didn't have any and giving a long rambling sum up of what we did and the dreams and vision God had put in our hearts, we were sent away with our tails between our legs.

I smiled, but to be honest, inside I felt grieved. Everyone around us was embarrassed. You could have heard a pin drop! I could feel my eyes welling up, and I was trying so hard to smile, walk in love and suck back the tears.

On the way to the hall, we were asked to be ushers. So for all the week of meetings we sat on the back row of the auditorium looking after our group. It was great and we were incredibly blessed!

So the voice of God (in the crowded room) said to me, 'Soon I will bring you out of the field, like David.' On the last night, the head usher pulled Samuel and me out from the back row. Thinking we were being given a task to perform, we followed.

I had really high heels on and going 'clonk, clonk, clonk', and feeling incredibly self-conscious, followed the usher. To my horror, we were then taken to the second to front row – in front of everyone in the auditorium!

Upon arriving, there was a painful silence as the usher bent down and whispered to the man at the end of the row with the empty seats. He looked at us, and then his nod said 'No' to the usher.

By this time the sweat was dripping from my brow and I looked like I had sunburn.

Samuel and I looked like something out of John Travolta's film 'Saturday Night Fever' – we had all white, snazzy outfits on. The usher then moved us to one side, and, as we were seated, we were then beckoned back to the other seats.

The speaker who was in mid-flow just looked at me and there we sat, wishing we were sitting on the back row. I am sure that God was laughing!

Anyway, about David in 1 Samuel 16:10: God commands Samuel to go and anoint one of Jesse's sons as king. After meeting with the sons he says that the Lord has not chosen any of them. So Samuel asks Jesse, 'Are these all there are?' Jesse says to him, 'Well there is the youngest, but he's out in the fields watching the sheep.'

King David was overlooked by his own family, and was out in the fields as a shepherd boy when God pinpointed him. David was anointed by Samuel as King, and still had to return to the fields to tend the sheep.

In 1 Samuel 17:17 we read of how David has a 'servant heart' and took food to his brothers who were in battle. Following that act of service, he is taken from the fields into the place where he slays Goliath.

Just imagine it: you have gone to take food to your brothers – and end up killing a giant. In 2 Samuel 17:34 David has to convince Saul that he is equipped and ready for the battle against Goliath by the experience he gained through protecting the sheep.

I love it!

God trained him in the fields – a place hidden away from the eyes of others – 'the school of life'. There was hope for me yet.

David went from being a shepherd boy … to a giant killer … to a king!

So the ordinary every-day responsibilities could be a place of preparation, and a simple act of service like taking someone a packed lunch could be a key to unlocking a door to an adventure!

I have been a bit of a 'blabber-mouth' in the past.

In my excitement I have told everyone about my dreams, and then felt stuck in a pit, or a prison, or given myself a real sense of pressure and of accountability.

Someone once told me not to share my dreams with anyone, and that I if did, not to expect them to understand.

I love Joseph – actually I think we all do. I remember one day buying my husband, Samuel, a 'wow-out-there-multi-coloured-shirt'. A man in the shop who knew Samuel laughed at me and said that he would never wear the shirt – but he did.

He wore it once and he did take some stick. I must admit it was a bit 'in your face', but it was fun! Everyone thought he was wearing it for a dare!

My husband is a big dreamer.

That is why I bought him the shirt! God loves big dreamers! God loved Joseph. He shared his dream with his brothers. He said to them in Genesis 37:7, 'Listen to this dream I had.'

I think at some time in our lives, like Joseph, we have shared a dream with others, and they had not received it as we thought they would. Actually, it has felt like they have trampled on it, or thrown a bucket of cold water on our fire!

Joseph was betrayed, disowned and sold as a slave by his brothers. He had a bumpy ride, including being unjustly punished for a crime he didn't commit. But he had a dream. Talk about going through it, but in everything he kept his attitude right. While he was in prison Pharaoh spoke such words of praise about him in Genesis 41:38 – 'Can we find anyone like this man, one in whom is the spirit of God?'

Joseph knew God, and his God, his King as in the case of Nehemiah, made a way. Joseph goes from a prison to a palace, and in both places had a dream and a destiny. I also had to keep hold of my dreams – whatever the circumstances.

I had pursued the counterfeit like Paul. What hope I found in the words of Paul when he says in Galatians 1:15-16 – 'God who set me apart from birth and called me.'

What a turn-around!

With all that history dealt with at Calvary, he knew he was set apart from the womb for a purpose. I was forgiven and free like Paul – set aside from birth and called.

But was I equipped?

I realised that in Jesus I am totally set free from every limitation because I have the Spirit without limit!

John 3:34 – 'For the one whom God has sent speaks the words of God, for God gives the Spirit without limit.'

All I had to do was trust in the Word and place everything in God's hands, walking in faithfulness.

I was often paralysed – held back from walking in the fulfilment of my dreams and destiny through fear about not doing the right thing.

I allowed the voice of unbelief, insecurities, rejection and pride to drown out the cry for me to sow my time and giftings. Instead I buried them under a mound of unbelief and selfishness.

The story of talents in Luke 19:11 with the three servants who were given money to put to work has always challenged me. Two invested the money and gained a return. One, through fear, buried the money and gained no return.

Finally I have realised that the greatest evidence of the existence of God is an abundance of fruit in our lives.

So many sermons, books, songs, ministries, businesses, relationships have been thought about, and thought about, and then thought about some more.

I had missed so many opportunities – all because I wasn't doing what the Word said. I often knew what I should do, or a need I could meet, but was then walking away and not doing anything about it.

James 1:22 – 'Do not merely listen to the word, and so deceive yourselves. Do what it says!'

Mark 4:8 – 'Still other seed fell on good soil. It came up, grew and produced a crop, multiplying thirty, sixty, or even a hundred times. Then Jesus said, "He who has ears to hear let him hear."'

I said to myself 'no more: no more believing all these lies – in Jesus my soil is rich! I will not hide my talents! I am deeply rooted in God! I will produce a harvest!'

I've been branded as a Jezebel.

Yep, I don't know how many times I have been called a Jezebel and how many times that I have ministered to other women given that as a name badge. And that's when I wasn't a prodigal – actually that's when I was at my most submissive.

I don't want to sound like I am being flippant by saying these things, but, quite honestly, just because I can put up a shelf, or don't like to bake bread has earned me the title in the past!

Fear of being a Jezebel plagued me for years and paralysed me walking in my destiny!

The whole 'women in ministry thing' has been a big one for me to get my head around. I am not a feminist; I like men to open doors, etc.

In actual fact once, whilst travelling on the London underground in a cabin full of men, a woman, who looked like she was about to give birth, got on the tube. Not one man gave up his seat for her. I stood up, pointed at them and gave them all a telling off – much to their shock!

One of the 'gentlemen' told me it was our fault and that we had wanted to be classed as equals. As an equal he had an equal right to the seat. Umm …

I think this is when I don't want to leave any contact details so that I can't be flooded with shiploads of correspondence pointing out the error of my ways.

After ten years of soul searching – with a head covering and without – I am encouraged about my destiny and calling by the women of the Bible:

Deborah was both a leader and a prophet in Judges 4–5; Miriam: the leader of a nation and a worship leader, dancer and prophetess in Micah 6:4 and Exodus 15:20; Anna: a prophetess and public speaker in Luke 2:36; Huldah: 2 Kings 22:14; Isaiah's wife: Isaiah 8:3; Philip's four daughters: Acts 21:9 (all prophetesses); Phoebe: a servant of the church in Romans 16:1; Priscilla: who was a teacher in Acts 18:26; Chloe: those of Chloe's household in 1 Corinthians 1:11; Dorcas who made robes in Acts 9:39.

I find such inspiration from the book of Esther.

She was a woman of destiny who had dealt with her past as an orphan peasant girl, and didn't walk around with all the baggage that could so easily have weighed her down (Esther 1:8).

She was a woman who could keep a secret (Esther 1:10). She was a woman who walked in the favour of God (Esther 2:9). She was a woman who could take advice (Esther 2:10). She was a woman who stayed calm in the face of a crisis (Esther 3:8). She was a woman of destiny – 'And you have come to a royal position for such a time as this' (Esther 4:14). She was a woman of courage (Esther 4:16). She was a woman who was prepared – 'On the third day Esther put on her royal robes and stood in the inner court of the palace, in front of the king's hall' (Esther 5:1). I am royalty in Jesus and made ready by His righteousness! She was a woman who was patient (Esther 5:7). She was a woman of great wisdom (Esther 7:3). She was a woman of integrity (Esther 8:6). She was a woman of no compromise (Esther 9:13). She was a woman who finished the race (Esther 9: 32).

Like Esther I want to finish the race.

God has been challenging me so much about keeping my eyes on Him and pressing on to Him and all the fullness of His outworking in and through my life.

Philippians 3:13 – 'I press on toward the goal to win the prize for which God has called me heavenwards in Christ Jesus.'

Esther went from being a peasant girl to a woman on a mission – 'And you have come to a royal position for such a time as this.'

Esther was used to protect and save her race – I want to be used to protect and save the lost.

In eternity there's no going back.

My dreams, my destiny, my hopes, my desires, my vision in reality are the out-workings of God in me, with me, for me and for His people.

I want to stand before Him and have Him say 'Well done my good and faithful servant', and I want to take as many with me as possible so that they can hear Him say the same to them.

Life anchored in Jesus is our wings, causing us to fly in our calling and destiny.

Isaiah 40:31 – 'But those who hope in the Lord will renew their strength. They will soar on wings like eagles; they will run and not grow weary, they will walk and not grow faint.'

Standing at the airport in the line about to board the plane, I began reading about Mary Magdalene in John 20:1-19 from an expanded translation by Kenneth S. Wuest.

'Now, on the first day of the week, Mary, the Magdalene, comes early while it is still dark to the tomb, and she sees the stone moved out of its place out of the tomb. Then she runs and comes to Simon Peter and to the other disciple of whom Jesus was fond and says to them, They took the Lord out of the tomb, and we do not know where they laid him. Then Peter and the other disciple went out and were going on their way to the tomb. Now, the two were running together. And the other disciple was running ahead more swiftly than Peter and came first to the tomb. And he intently gazes upon the strips of linen cloth lying there and the handkerchief which had been upon His head, not lying with the strips of linen cloth, but apart, rolled up in one place. Then therefore went in also the other disciple who had come first to the tomb, and he saw and believed, for not yet did they know the scripture that it is a necessity in the nature of the case for Him to stand up [arise] out from among those who are dead. Then the disciples went off again to their own homes.

But Mary continued standing, facing the tomb, outside, weeping audibly. Then as she was weeping, she stooped down and looked into the tomb, and she carefully observes two angels in brilliant white garments sitting, one facing the head and one facing the feet, where the body of Jesus had been lying. And those say to her, Woman, why are you weeping? She says to them, They took away my Lord, and I do not know where they laid Him.

Having said these things, she turned herself back and carefully observes Jesus standing, and she did not know that it was Jesus. Jesus says to her, Woman, why are you weeping? Whom are you seeking? That one, thinking that it was the gardener, says to Him, Sir as for you, if you carried Him off, tell me at once where you laid Him, and, as for myself, I will carry Him off. Jesus says to her, Mary. That one, having turned around, says to Him in Hebrew, Rabboni, (which is to say, Teacher).'

Key words lodge themselves in my being, penetrating my heart:

Having said these things she turned herself back and carefully observed Jesus standing and she did not know that it was Jesus.

Jesus says to her, 'Woman, why are you weeping? Whom are you seeking?' 'That one, thinking it was the gardener', (she) says to Him, 'Sir as for you, if you carried Him off, tell me at once where you laid Him, and as for myself, I will carry him off.'

Jesus says to her, 'Mary.' That one, having turned around, says to Him in Hebrew, 'Rabboni' (which is to say, Teacher).

There was such passion, such a depth of intimate love in the words, I was so moved that tears were flowing uncontrollably down my face.

Jesus says to her, 'Mary!' Jesus had already spoken to her 'Woman, why are you weeping?' Why did she not know him? She knew the title 'woman' was not rude or derogatory – just the normal address. Yet also, before, people would call her 'that woman who had seven devils cast out'.

But when He said, 'Mary!' she turned. She knew that familiar voice. John 10:2 – 'The man who enters by the gate is the shepherd of the sheep. The watchman opens the gate for him, and the sheep listen to his voice. He calls his own sheep by name and leads them out.' Mary turns around and says to him in Hebrew 'Rabboni' (my master, teacher). She knew the voice of the one who loved her completely.

She had said; 'If you carried him off, tell me at once as for myself I will carry him off.' She went to the tomb disappointed and grieving but knowing His love: so high you can't get over it; so wide you can't get around it, so deep you can't get under it. Oh, wonderful love!

She said she would carry him off, and she did in her heart, her life and her everything!

I want to carry him from the North to the South, to the East and the West.

Do you?

I'm flying

'but for you who revere my name, the sun of
righteousness will rise with healing in its wings.'

malachi 4:2

Photography: richard farquhar

'my faith was strengthened

by frankie creith

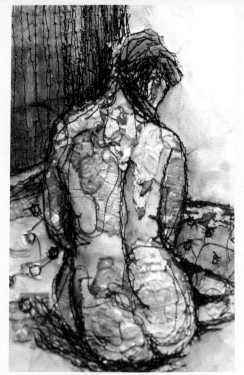

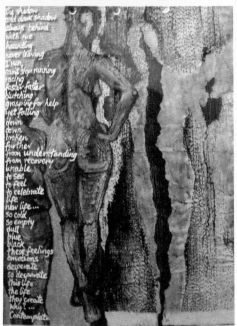

'It is impossible for me to divorce my Christian faith from my creative journey,' says wife, mother and artist Frankie Creith.

For Frankie, who has been a professional artist for seventeen years since graduating with a BA Hons. in fine craft design, specialising in embroidery - the journey has been one of God-discovery and subsequent self-discovery.

After a period of ten years striving for recognition, Frankie used her art as a means of therapy as she walked through two years of anxiety and depression.

'Although I had accepted Jesus as my personal Lord and Saviour, I had put Him to the bottom of my priorities as I strove towards my self-set goals,' she says. Frankie knew at this point that God had called her to give Him His rightful place in her life and art. 'It was an overwhelming realisation and one that I could not ignore,' she says.

Mathew 6: 33
'Seek first the kingdom of God and His righteousness, and all these things shall be added to you.'

Turning from selfish ambition, her desire was now to glorify God in her art. Since this intense realisation and life changing experience, God has made a way and opened many doors.

Frankie has been encouraged through the word of God, especially from Exodus 26: 1 'Make the tabernacle with 10 curtains of finely twisted linen and blue, purple and scarlet yarn, with cherubim worked into them by a skilled craftsman.'

'I believed that this same God who is as real and living today as He was then would instruct me as I work - and He has! His presence was very real to me as I worked, and my faith was strengthened,' she says.

Now two pieces of her work are displayed in a London museum's permanent textile collection. The catalogue statement about her work rejoices in the scripture – Romans 6:28 'The gift of God is eternal life.'

Frankie has experienced personally that by placing God central in her life and work, He has enabled her to achieve immeasurably more than she could ever have imagined.

John 10:10
'I have come that they may have life, and that they may have it more abundantly.'

photography: andy hill frankie creith: frankiejhill@hotmail.com

family owned 200 year old farmyard site farmyard site

family owned 200 year old farmyard si

6000 sq ft

6000 sq ft

6000 sq ft

sq

local stonemasons

stone

Kathy architect architect

years

two

**two
years
to
build**

years

oneyear

one year to design by Kathy

renovated old and new building combined contemporary farmhouse look

belfast roof materials salvaged from crumlin mill in belfast   salvaged

crumlin mill   crumlin

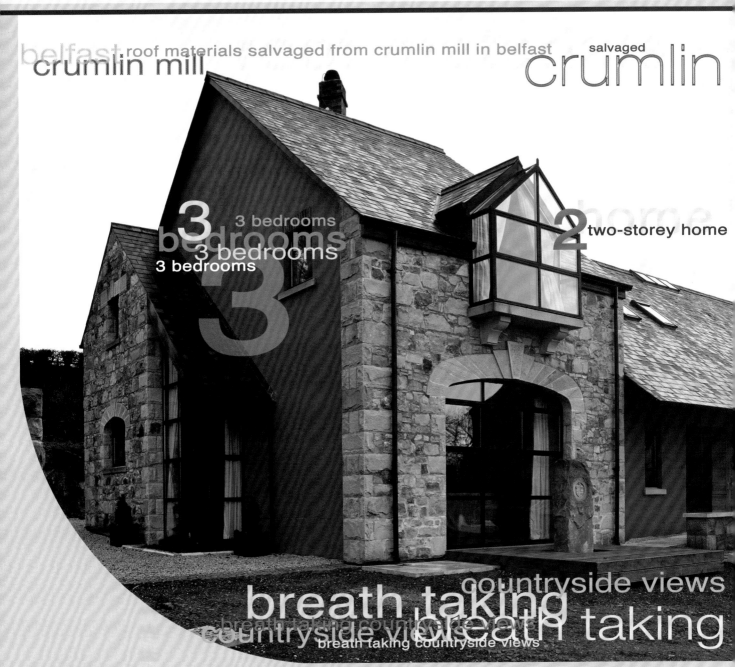

3
3 bedrooms
bedrooms
3 bedrooms
3 bedrooms
3

2 two-storey home

countryside views
breath taking   breath taking
breath taking countryside views
countryside views
breath taking countryside views

warmth

open fire

american walnut

love

warm tones

space

relaxed

soft furnishings

entertaining

candles

open plan

honed

marble

floor

comfort

family

home

Isaiah 32:18
'My people shall
dwell in a
peaceable habitation,
in safe dwelling,
and in quiet
resting — places.

oak-clad ceilings
oak
ceilings

wall carrying
through entire house
entire house

local sandstone
sandstone
stone

rich colour **rich** *colours*
rich colours

dark walnut floors *floors*
dark

marble
italian marble
italian marble

aluminium-clad units - star galaxy granite worktop - jura grey marble floor
colourful art - south facing rooms - natural light - built in griddle
steam oven - three-tier glass design - family
hub of house - comfortable

art
canvas

sandstone
sandstone

original art

combined
glass
steel
glass and steel

marble
marble treads

marble treads

family

music
jura
jura gold marble

gold
marble
music

piano

family

original art

music

space - bed - dress - bath

soft bedding

crocodile brown pattern

upholstered headboard

leather wall covering

plump pillows textures

vibrant colour

feathers

lamps

photography: paul sherwood www.sherwood.ie

twin sink

rich wood

en-suite bathroom

natural light

his & her
walk in dressing rooms

main bathroom

lavish bathing

simple lines

jura gold marble

walnut
surround

photography: richard farquhar

1 / B 8 / H12 /

97608340 0440

82997608340 0440

9 /

ND

if the 4 walls could speak –

what would they say?

life?

laughter?

love?

living stones

A Victoria Sandwich Cake with Steve and Danielle

I was at a Christian barbeque, stuffing my face with a gorgeous, succulent, homemade burger, covered in blue cheese and onions, when a vivacious girl, full of life, told me about her Pastors - Steve from Holland and Danielle from Australia. "They stood upon God's Word, His provision, His promise and He brought them here. Our Church meets in their house; it's a great Church and a wonderful place to fellowship. They have got really good taste and a wonderful gift in hospitality; you would love them," she said.

Their testimony unfolded through the lips of someone who had been watching them and listening. Wow! What a witness they must have been to her, and she was to me. Steve and Danielle were obviously people full of faith, as they had left their home with their children to follow the call of God in their lives.

Led by God, they had bought a run down old property in Desertmartin, County Londonderry three and a half years ago. After living in it for two years, God prompted them to clear the site and build a new house. The girl was full of such admiration for the couple, her words and zeal made a huge impact upon my memory.

The following month, whilst on a trip to America, God kept pressing me to contact Steve and Danielle and ask them if they would invite us into their home. So, after a night flight, I called and arranged to meet them that evening. Samuel my hubby was my chauffeur, and armed with my red eye special eye drops, we drove down a country lane into a sweeping driveway to their detached property. Nice house, I thought; wonder what it's like inside?

Have you ever had one of those experiences when you meet someone and it's like you have known them all your life: even their home feels familiar? This was one such occasion. Actually I will let you into a little secret; we were so tired, but having such a great time talking, we didn't want to go. Our body clocks were all over the place, and my husband fell asleep in the middle of a conversation with Steve! We left: piled high with Joyce Meyer's teaching tapes from the Church library.

24hrs later

Still jet lagged, I turned up on their doorstep with a cafetiere, coffee and a huge, fresh cream, Victoria sandwich cake. Danielle welcomed me at the door with a smile and big hug. I walked into the lounge, and as I looked through to the kitchen I heard a snigger. I saw my photographer, very comfortable I might add, sitting at the breakfast bar enjoying a freshly brewed cuppa.

It was Danielle's day off work: she works at a dental clinic as a marketing / care consultant. Danielle's organisational skills and methodical mind are apparent in the attention to detail given in the construction, layout and finishing of the house. "We prayed over every plan, and thanked God for His wisdom in choosing the right tradesmen, suppliers and for positive responses from council authorities," says Danielle.

With flowing open plan living and lots of windows, the house is spacious and airy. Steve's window cleaning business ensures all the rooms are flooded with light through the sparkling glass. Being self-employed gives him the freedom to Pastor the church and be like the apostle Paul who used his tent making to earn a wage. Steve popped home and shared his experience of building from scratch, as well as a cup of tea and a slice or two of the Victoria sponge cake. "We made sure that quality materials were used on the major structure of the home. We cut no corners when it came to windows, outside doors and insulation," says Steve.

A place to relax

The neutral walls provide a blank canvas for art, rich coloured furnishings and accessories. "I love to snuggle up on our comfortable corner sofa with a pot of tea and just chill out with Christian friends," says Danielle. The room is open, yet warm and inviting, silk cushions bring additional splashes of colour. The solid wooden coffee table with wicker baskets is great for neat, trendy storage. "The room is evolving and we think that we might take the plunge and add a bit of colour to a couple of walls next," says Danielle.

"It's great to have an open plan house. I can put my feet up in the lounge and call through to the kitchen for a cuppa," says Danielle.

photography: steve thompson - www.stevethompsonphotography.co.uk

Nathan accessorises the kitchen wall with his masterpiece.

The hub of the home

Two teenagers with healthy appetites means a well-equipped kitchen with lots of cupboard space was a must. "Because we are taller than most people we had our wooden kitchen worktops raised by three inches," says Steve. The light cream units are timeless, and complement the airy feel. Additional lighting over the breakfast bar was needed because of the overall size of the room. This is the hub of the house and the swivelling bar stools are great for an easy manoeuvre when turning to chat to through traffic from the lounge. A solid wooden table and chairs adds warmth to the room. Original pieces of artwork scatter the walls; coloured dishes with fruit or vegetables are strategically placed on the freshly oiled worktops.

Steve and Nathan chill out and enjoy father — son time in the kitchen.

Plump pillows and crisp white bedding.

Sweet dreams

A bright hallway and open plan staircase lead to the downstairs
master bedroom. A khaki wall is the backdrop to a large
comfortable bed, with plump pillows and fresh, crisp bedding.
The room is spacious and a walk in wardrobe provides ample
space for clothing and shoes. "We like to spend time in the
word before we go to sleep," says Danielle. Two bedside tables
with pretty matching lamps give soft lighting to the eyes.

Luxury ensuite shower room

"It's great to have a large cupboard under the sink to hide away all our toiletries and spare toilet rolls," says Danielle. A large mirror over the sinks reflects the light keeping the room bright.

Two sinks means that the romantic couple can clean their teeth at the same time!

vibrant lime green silk cushion

Feminine chic

Hotel feel bathroom

Feminine chic

Tiffany's inherited Mum's design flare. Cream coloured walls are contrasted with the rich colours of luxurious fabrics and accessories. Deep burgundy voiles and light shade, purple silk cushions and a golden silk throw make this room incredible feminine. An old - style reproduction bed sits under a Velux window and is in a sea of art. A radiator is hidden by Tiffany's masterpiece: flowers that combine all of the colours in the room.   An elegant dark wood chair with a vibrant lime green silk cushion is a great place for her to kick off her shoes and be still.

Hotel feel bathroom

Danielle is pleased because she has created a hotel look bathroom at a reasonable price. An oval shaped bath, enclosed with tiled sides and walls, sits set back next to the corner shower unit. A Velux window allows light to pour into this well planned and tastefully decorated room.

Every inch of Steve and Danielle's three bedroom home is lived in and incredibly organised with all the space well planned and used. The landing doubles up as an open plan office and study centre with a selection of Christian authors and study guides. With 2 grown up kids, a church to pastor and a business, this home is a hive of activity. The foundations of this house and home are the usual concrete, but also a firm base of prayer, worship and Bible.

This home and the family's lives are a testimony to 'The Lord is my shepherd, I shall not lack.' They stepped out in faith and walked in fearless confidence in the promises of God.

his lovingkindne

I didn't see God as He is.

I don't know if I am the only person in the world who has been disturbed and troubled at some point in time by a nagging unease about the character of God. Dodgy, wonky doctrine and thinking tagged onto some of life's knocks and lows left me with a false image of God.

It may be shocking to admit but, to be honest, I saw God as sadistic, waiting around every corner with a big stick and the threat of eternal damnation. I had seen God as unpredictable, angry and waiting for me to step out of line so that he could punish and reject me.

Duh! What I had believed couldn't have been further from the truth. Now I am smiling inside because I know personally what the word says – that God is good.

Give thanks to the Lord, for He IS GOOD; For His lovingkindness is everlasting (Psalm 118:1).

In the Hebrew – the word good means that our God is pleasant, beautiful, excellent, lovely, delightful, close by, joyful, fruitful, precious, sound, cheerful, kind, correct, righteous, the good, the right, virtue, happiness and moral goodness.

ss is everlasting

And our good God will never stop doing good to us (Jeremiah 32:40).

Our father in heaven gives us good gifts (Matthew 7:11).

Well that straightened a few things out and I could give thanks to the Lord for He is good; For His lovingkindness is everlasting (Psalm 118:1).

His lovingkindness is *everlasting*

God's lovingkindness is an attitude of love that contains mercy. It's a love of kindness, favour, grace, loyalty, beauty and it's unfailing.

One day walking along the beach I told God how much I had been plagued with a fear of Him rejecting me. He showed me that He was my source of salvation. I realised that my salvation was based purely upon His grace and not my own efforts. I could not add or take away from the finished work of Calvary; instead I was to rest in it.

his lovingkindne

But because of His great love for us, God, who is rich in mercy, made us alive with Christ even when we were dead in transgressions – it is by grace you have been saved. And God raised us up with Christ and seated us with Him in heavenly realms in Christ Jesus, in order that in the coming ages He might show the incomparable riches of grace, expressed in his lovingkindness to us in Christ Jesus. For it is by grace you have been saved, through faith – and this not from yourselves, it is the gift of God – not by works, so that no-one can boast. For we are God's workmanship, created in Christ Jesus to do good works, which God prepared in advance for us to do (Ephesians 2:4–10).

I returned home different that day. I returned home with a message of good news! I had a peace that I had never experienced before. God loved me and forgave my sins because He wanted to!

I no longer set myself up as an idol who thought she could make it all happen by her works. No longer did I have to strive to accomplish not missing the mark. Instead I could rest in His grace, His free gift to me. I bubble inside with His love and acceptance and overflowed with it, knowing that God came to demonstrate that He is for us and not against us (Romans 8:31)!

Now I have a quiet confidence, like a child trusting in its parent's unconditional love. God is my source of salvation!

The Lord is for me; I will not fear (Psalm 118:6).

But God demonstrates His own love for us in this. While we were still sinners, Christ died for us (Romans 5:8).

ss is everlasting

These scriptures set me free from believing that God was waiting to catch me out so that He could reject me. I saw the heart of my loving God who so desired relationship with me.

It's great to rest in the knowledge that God's love is always unselfish, active compassion towards us that endures forever.

For God so loved the World that He gave His only begotten Son that whoever believes in Him shall not perish but have eternal life (John 3:16).

I want to jump for joy knowing that His lovingkindness is everlasting!

Give thanks to the Lord for He is good; for His lovingkindness is everlasting (Psalm 118:1).

I can do cartwheels now because I know that God's lovingkindness is consistent, forever, eternal, everlasting, without end – mercy, grace, loyalty, beauty and unfailing love.

I tell you the truth he who believes has everlasting life (John 6:47).

his lovingkindne

For a long time I had to renew my mind, and break the habit and the memory of the lie I had believed for so long. Every time there was doubt I would remind myself that God has married me forever.

For your maker is your husband, the Lord almighty is his name (Isaiah 54:5). Instead of a fear of rejection, I thought about the lovingkindness of God.

Rejoice in the Lord always. I will say it again: Rejoice! Let your gentleness be evident to all. The Lord is near. Do not be anxious about anything, but in everything, by prayer and petition, with thanksgiving, present your requests to God. And the peace of God will guard your hearts and your minds in Christ Jesus. Finally, brothers, whatever is true, whatever is noble, whatever is right, whatever is pure, whatever is lovely, whatever is admirable – if anything is excellent or praiseworthy – think about such things (Philippians 4:4).

I had to deal with the memory and life experience of rejection and not reflect this upon the character of God. As a child of God fear or rejection and eternal separation from God was a lie: a habit of thought I changed through the reality and the promise of the word, by renewing my mind and thinking about the lovingkindness of God.

ss is everlasting

Do not conform any longer to the patterns of this world, but be transformed by the renewing of your mind. Then you will be able to test and approve what God's will is – His good, pleasing and perfect will (Romans 12:2).

I was transformed by my 'love-truth' thoughts.

Our partners may have left us, our parents may have disowned us, our children may have forgotten us, and our friends may have shelved us but not our God!

Can a mother forget the baby at her breast and have no compassion on the child she has borne? Though she may forget you! See, I have engraved you on the palms of my hands (Isaiah 49:15).

The songwriter Augustus Toplady wrote:
'My name from the palms of His hand
Eternity will not erase;
Impressed upon His heart it remains,
In marks of indelible grace.'

God does not forget us – He eternally cherishes us and he carries our photo like a tattoo on the palms of His hands.

his lovingkindne

I tell you, whoever acknowledges me before men, the Son of Man will also acknowledge him before the angels of God (Luke 12:8).

I am pretty sure that God shows me off like a proud father to all the angels! Like a dad presenting a photo of his child to a friend.

I tell you, there is rejoicing in the presence of the angels of God over one sinner who repents (Luke 15:10).

Yep! My God is a proud dad showing off the apple of His eyes, His daughter!

My 'abba-dad' is a perfect father (Matthew 5:48).

He shows me compassion: in the Hebrew compassion is to touch or stroke someone gently in a loving or affectionate way, to soothe, to cherish, to love deeply, to show pity, to be tender, to demonstrate mercy, a womb, compassion, sympathy, tenderness, sensitive love.

God gives us, from His very hand, every good gift we receive (James 1:17).

ss is everlasting

How much more shall your Father who is in heaven give what is good to those who ask Him! (Matthew 7:11).

My good, loving-kind, eternal God comforts me in all my troubles
(2 Corinthians 1:3–4).
And He is my greatest encourager
(2 Thessalonians 2:16–17).

God called me by name and I am His (Isaiah 43:1).

He even knows the very hairs on my head are numbered (Matthew 10:29–31). And the grey ones!

So I can give thanks to the Lord, for He is good, for His lovingkindness is everlasting.

To give thanks in the Hebrew means to hold out the hand, to revere or worship with extended hands, to confess, praise, to shout.

I am smiling inside – knowing God is good.

I give thanks to the Lord for He is good;
For His lovingkindness is everlasting.

As a **Christian architect**, **Alan Jones** takes personal inspiration and direction from the many parts of the Bible that mention construction and building. Reasons why he has become an architect and what role he should play in the world are suggested by Ezekiel 40 v 3 & 4:

Divine Inspiration

'...and I saw a man whose appearance was like bronze: He was standing in the gateway with a linen cord and a measuring rod in his hand. The man said to me, "Son of man, look with your eyes and hear with your ears and pay attention to everything I am going to show you, for that is why you have been brought here..."'

'When I am practising as an architect or teaching, I think and ask, 'Why I am here, doing what I am doing, and how can I maximise the impact of what I do?'

'To me, architects can be like angels in society. They can look at the world and observe how life can be changed and improved by the simplest of moves and strategies. Educated initially as problem-solvers, architects have the potential to take solutions and translate them from basic functionalism to the finer qualities of beauty, simplicity and grace," says Alan.

He and his wife Laura have created a new house and home for themselves and their two boys – twelve year old Isaac and ten year old Gideon - in a small town twenty miles north of Belfast.

Back in 2002, while reading a local newspaper, an advertisement for a 0.8 acre empty site, with outline planning permission for a single house, caught their eye. They were very excited - the site was exactly what they had been looking for and in a perfect location. Laura's mind was already dreaming about their new home, but upon enquiring about the sale they were told that the vendor had already accepted an offer. Most people would have just given up and looked for something else, but they knew that they were destined to own the land and build their own house on it.   Twelve months later they received a long awaited call - the sale had fallen through and their offer had been accepted!

So what made the site so special?
'We had been used to urban living with our seven years in Camden, London – and this site, next to a series of public buildings, is as urban as a small Ulster town can be. It is close to church, school, shopping and the local rugby club and scout hall. Many in Ulster aspire to country living – but for us the site presented a great opportunity for town living with all the advantages that brings,' says Laura.

'We still have our countryside - the adjacent stream, the existing, extensive mature boundary planting and the views towards the Antrim Hills and Slemish Mountain all ensure that, although urban, nature is here also,' says Alan.

With the setting in mind Alan went about designing their new family home to complement both the urban and the natural.

'I was influenced largely by an Old Congregation Presbyterian Church, a well-known local landmark. As one of only two oval churches in Ireland, this Grade A listed church is an architectural jewel,' says Alan.

Design Approach

Alan's immediate design aim was to create a dwelling that was visually quiet and recessive, with no light-coloured components that would distract a viewer from the listed church.

'The black stone and white window frames of the listed building are very impressive at night, with a lantern-type image when the internal lights are on,' says Alan.

Observing this encouraged Alan to ensure his design was the opposite – muted, dark and visually quiet – with only a single, tall gable window illuminated at night.

In response to the narrow nature of the site and its context, the new house presents a gable to the public road, in the same way as the other buildings next to the listed church. The tall, narrow window on the roadside gable is of a civic/public scale, an architectural feature which enhances the ambiguous nature of the design.

Surely it's not a house!
'We wanted a house that fitted in with its surroundings when looking from the road and churchyard. Instead of looking like a house, we wanted it to look more like a public or civic building. We finally finished the construction in March 2004, and the design has been so successful in this regard that the locals could not decide if it was a hotel, a church or a church hall,' laughs Laura.

churchyard

From the churchyard to the side and rear of the listed church, the house presents tall 'one-sided' bay-windows, again being public and civic in scale. When leaving the listed church from the side door adjacent to the house, the blank sides of these bay windows are visible, but there is no view into the house. Church-goers are not distracted by views into a domestic property, and only see a sombre outline with no illumination.

The gradual slope of the site made it seem obvious to Alan to lift the house slightly off the site at the front, and to slip a basement garage and utility room underneath – and align the ground floor level with the rear external south-facing deck. It was also fortuitous that south was away from the public road, and initial sketches showed that public north and private south was a theme that began almost instantly.

It is only when one moves around to the rear private garden and views the south elevation that the house begins to take on a domestic scale.

This is the view that the only neighbouring house has of our dwelling. A large timber deck is next to the rear elevation, taking advantage of the sun from early morning through to evening.

'I love to spend time here with the family in the summer months – it's a great place for barbeques.' says Alan.

The first entrance door one approaches has an external screen that masks the second and more private entrance further along the side elevation. Immediately inside the home, small spaces and the main stair are placed along the side of the house. The front entrance leads to the guest WC, study and main reception room and dining room.

'I take pleasure in the large, open ground-floor space, which suits our gregarious nature,' says Laura.

Inside the house, the light, views and the textured concrete are in contrast to the dark, smooth exterior. Each morning, as soon as the sun rises over the churchyard wall, the house is filled with sunlight, which stays until the evening.

The tall windows facing south are where the family sit to read, have breakfast or just daydream, looking out towards the stream, churchyard and sky.

'our house has sunshine inside'

With low ceiling heights in proportion to the size of the rooms, this gave a clear zone under the first floor structure for servicing the bathroom and ensuites above. Each of the taller, larger spaces on the ground floor has one of the side bay windows, offering beautiful views and a bright sunlit space. Throughout the house there are voids to the roof, accepting that trees and banks to the sides of the site restrict the ingress of natural light at certain times. The voids also allow the extent of the concrete perimeter walls to be understood and appreciated as an artistic feature.

Like the church next door, the interior cannot be read from the exterior. In both cases there is reward for entering. The church reveals a wonderful ox-bowl balcony, and the house reveals brightly-lit textured, concrete perimeter walls, and plain plastered walls forming low, medium and tall spaces.

The scale of the front room of the house feels like that of a hotel lobby, continuing the ambiguity of the outside public scale, yet for a private dwelling - an ideal space to receive guests or a visiting minister.

Looking at the plan, it appears as if the house has been ruffled and shaken to remove any staid formalism, creating a spatial dynamism that continues to reveal itself as you walk through and sit to enjoy the interior. Above the basement garage and utility, the ground floor has small intimate spaces placed to one side with the main spaces set together forming one long space over 65 feet long and 18ft wide - an ideal place for entertaining large groups of people. Necessary doors appear from walls to segregate areas, but glass over-panels continue the visual connection from gable to gable.

With hidden sliding and hinged doors, this space can be closed down and made into a series of smaller, more private rooms.

Thus the family have an open plan area or they have rooms - when they want them.

Having designed a number of private one-off houses, Alan has become increasingly frustrated with the common mix of masonry and steel structures that subsequently require plastering – with the mess, cost and risk of cracking that can occur. Looking to the remnants of old buildings and structures, Alan saw that a permanent perimeter structure of 'in situ' concrete provided the internal structural stability and flexibility. Floors spanning wall-to-wall provided an extensive, exposed thermal mass which co-ordinated with his energy strategy for the building.

'Externally insulating the form and covering in a rain screen construction allowed a relaxed approach to detailing and the process of building', says Alan.

The concrete perimeter walls were formed with OSB boards, leaving a surface impression which is soft and semi natural, linking the interior to the natural exterior beyond.

The interior of the house feels dramatic and spacious, yet relaxed and informal. A mix of furniture, including design classics, and contrasting white and bright colours complement the raw concrete walls.

'the house feels dramatic and spacious'

Forming a skeletal shell, the exposed concrete walls and the polished concrete floors create an immense thermal store which, once warmed by the geothermal heating system, gives a stable thermal environment, warm in winter and cool in summer.

The stairs from basement to the first floor bedroom accommodation are off the second, more private, entrance hall at the rear of the house.

HEBREWS 3:4 'For every house is built by someone, but God is the builder of everything.'

The house has created much discussion locally, with strangers asking the family how they are enjoying it.

'I am told school children sit in buses deciding who likes it and who does not,' says Laura.

People often tell Laura they are so pleased that they have built on the site and are delighted with what has been built.

'Our visitors book has such comments as "Your new house appears to have always been here" and "It is the right answer" says Alan.

'I particularly remember and agree with one comment that the design is "strangely familiar" in that different people see different things in the design, but cannot quite put their finger on what it is. I suppose that is what architecture is - different things to different people, evoking memories and past images', says Alan.

The family feel that the design is right and they look forward to many years enjoying their new home.

www.jonesarchitects.com

Blue skies, smiling on me
Nothing but blue skies do I see
Blue birds singing a song
Nothing but blue skies from now on.

artwork: mark case, www.whitenoisestudios.com

he will rejoice ove

As a little girl my mum and dad always called me their little princess. When I was about five a lady told me that I was beautiful. Twirling around with flowing hands, I replied, 'I know, for my mummy told me so.' Yes, you have guessed it! I have never lived this down! To the lady I must have seemed like a precocious little brat!

Reflecting on this today, it tickles and challenges me. My ma and pa said I was beautiful and I believed it. If only I had been like that with God. So often we believe He thinks the worst about us. So often we don't see ourselves as He sees us. As His daughter, I believe that when the Father looks at me He sees Jesus and His perfection.

Now I am a 37 year old, 10 stone twinkle toes, twirling around with flowing hands and smiling inside I can say, 'I am beautiful for my 'abba-daddy' says so.' He said it and 'finally' I now actually believe it!

The Lord, your God is in your midst, a mighty saviour; He will rejoice over you with gladness, and renew you in his love; He will sing joyfully because of you, as one sings at festivals (Zephaniah 3:17 New American Bible).

design by www.markflint.net

you with singing

My good, loving-kind, eternal God is 'In the midst of me' – God is with me. The Hebrew word for midst means 'the nearest part, the centre, among, before, bowels and heart'. Finally I got it. My God was not aloof and far off, but He is ever present and is right here now.

I love the story in 1 Kings 19 about Elijah. He goes from having such triumph and victory over the prophets of Baal at Mount Carmel, to being threatened by Jezebel and becoming afraid and running away.

From a mountain top experience to falling flat on his face! I think we all can relate to this in some way. So there he is running away like a chicken and the Lord meets with him, sends ravens to feed him and gives him peace, quiet and restoration.

The Lord said, Go out and stand on the mountains in the presence of the Lord, for the Lord is about to pass by. Then a great and powerful wind tore the mountains apart and shattered the rocks before the Lord, but the Lord was not in the wind. After the wind there was an earthquake, but the Lord was not in the earthquake. After the earthquake came a fire. And after the fire came a gentle whisper (1 Kings 19:11). What a loving-kind God!

A gentle whisper, quiet, peace and restoration. That's not forgetting the cake, hopefully chocolate! It's great to know that I don't have to wait for God to pass by. I live under the new covenant; Jesus is my Lord and Saviour and I am one with Him! But he who unites himself with the Lord is one with him in spirit (1 Corinthians 6:17).

he will rejoice ove

Yahweh your God is there with you, the warrior saviour. He will rejoice over you with happy song, he will renew you by his love, he will dance with shouts of joy for you, as on a day of festival (New Jerusalem bible).

My God is a Saviour [who saves]! God is mighty to save: a warrior and a mighty-saviour. In the Hebrew, warrior means that our Saviour is a powerful champion, chief, giant. He is mighty, strong, valiant.

God is mighty to save – He gives victory. He defends us, delivers us, helps us, preserves us, rescues us, makes us safe, brings (having) salvation, saves and is victory.

Shouts of joy and victory resound in the tents of the righteous; The Lord's right hand had done mighty things. (Psalm 118:15 NIV) The New American Standard version says 'The right hand of the Lord does valiantly.'

Our good, loving-kind, eternal, ever-present God is being busy – providing, serving, defending and active with His right hand. For us! He is our military might. He is our strength and our army. Who is the King of Glory? The Lord strong and mighty, the Lord mighty in battle (Psalm 24:8).

Did you know that the Lord laughs at the wicked for He knows their day is coming? (Psalm 37:13). I make myself laugh, ha-ha-ha, at all that comes against me. If God is being busy on my behalf and He is laughing, then I laugh with Him!

The Lord your God is with you, He is mighty to save. He will take great delight in you, He will quiet you with His love (Zephaniah 3:17).

you with singing

The Lord delights in us. Our good, loving-kind, eternal, ever-present, warrior-Saviour delights in us.

I love my little dog. She is beautiful to me. The other day I bathed her, tied her hair in pink bows and fastened her new trend-setting, pink, feathery collar around her now sweet-smelling fury neck. Clothed in her matching stripy pink and white funky coat, her tail was wagging and I was so happy. It had been raining outside, and knowing how much she hates getting her feet wet, I carried her in her special designer, pretty pink princess bag. We both delighted in the experience!

Our God experiences delight, joy and pleasure through a relationship with us. So, delight yourselves in the Lord and He will give you the desires of your heart. Commit your way to the Lord. Trust also in him and He will do it (Psalm 37:4). As God delights in us, He also desires us to delight in Him. It's great to know that the Lord delights in making us prosperous (Deut 30:9), that God rescues us because he delights in us (2 Samuel 22:20), and that God comforts us because He delights in us (Isaiah 65:19).

The Lord your God is with you; He is mighty to save; He will take great delight in you; He will quiet you with his love; He will rejoice over you with singing (Zephaniah 3:17 NIV).

he will rejoice ove

Our good, loving-kind, eternal, ever-present God delights in us, quiets and renews us. God quiets us and renews us. He causes us to be still, at peace and at rest. Be still and know that I am God (Psalm 46:10).

I love the story in Luke 8:24 where Jesus goes out in a boat with the disciples and tells them that they are going to the other side. There is a violent storm and the disciples panic, but Jesus gets up and rebukes the wind and the raging waters; the storm subsided and all was calm.

Like he calmed the storm for the disciples Jesus hushes the storms in our lives, emotions and minds when we rest in his love. In God's love we are calmed, stilled, quieted, renewed and we live, recover, are revived, nourished and preserved.

I shall not die but live and tell the works of the Lord (Psalm 118:17). Abundant living – Jesus was sent to bind up the broken-hearted, proclaim freedom for the captives, release from darkness for the prisoners, to proclaim the year of the Lord's favour, to comfort all who mourn, to provide for those who grieve, to give beauty where there was ashes, gladness instead of morning and praise instead of despair (Isaiah 61).

Our good, loving-kind, eternal, ever-present, warrior-Saviour, delights in us, quiets us and revives us with His love – His friendship, familiar love and covenant loyalty.

In 1 Corinthians 13:8 the Lord tells us that love never fails and in 1 John 4:18 that His love is perfect and casts out fear. What a beautiful love letter Jesus is!

you with singing

I pray that out of His glorious riches He may strengthen you with power through His spirit in your inner being, so that Christ may dwell in your hearts through faith. And I pray that, you being rooted and established in love, may have power together with all the saints, to grasp how wide and long and high and deep is the love of Christ, and to know this love – that you may be filled to the measure of all the fullness of God (Ephesians 3:16).

God quiets and revives us in His love as we become rooted and established in the fullness of it, desiring that we would live in the overflow of the heartfelt knowledge that He is love.

God sees and values us as His treasured possession (Exodus 19:5). He desires to lavish His love upon us (1 John 3:1). He has brought me to his banquet hall, and his banner over me is love (Songs of Songs 2:4,5).

God has brought us to his banquet hall and His banner over us is love. It's time to feast upon the love of God.

The Lord your God is in the midst of you, a Mighty one, a Saviour [Who saves]! He will rejoice over you with joy; He will rest [in silent satisfaction] and in His love He will be silent and make no mention [of past sins, or even recall them]; He will exult over you with singing (Zephaniah 3:17 Amp).

I used to walk around with a heavy heart, so focused on my sin. Now I have twinkle toes and I dance, focused upon His love, His grace and His forgiveness. When I make a mistake I say 'sorry' and I am quiet and revived in His mercy. His love covers all transgressions (Proverbs 10:12).

he will rejoice ove

The Lord your God is with you, He is mighty to save. He will take great delight in you, He will quiet you with his love, He will rejoice over you with singing (Zephaniah 3:17).

Our good, loving-kind, eternal, ever-present, warrior-Saviour, delights in us and rejoices over us.

The other day I was driving my car singing away, belting it out – quite some noise, believe me! I suddenly realised that I had totally missed my exit on the motorway and had driven another 20 minutes. I was so focused on God, so caught up in the moment, that all my thoughts had shifted onto how amazing He is and how much He loves me. It was like time had stood still; unfortunately it hadn't and I was late for my date with my husband!

The fuller meaning of the Hebrew word 'rejoice' means that our God spins around under the influence of a violent emotion rejoicing! Yippee! Our God rejoices over us with gladness – with happy song as the New Jerusalem Bible says.

Our God spins around over us (above, among, over, touching) with a happy song – with loud singing and with shouts of joy. He is singing!

you with singing

The Lord my God is with me. He is mighty to save. He takes great delight in me; He quiets me with his love; He rejoices over me with singing (Zephaniah 3:17).

But for you who revere my name, the sun of righteousness will rise with healing in its wings. And you will go out and leap like calves released from the stall (Malachi 4:2).

I have twinkle toes; I dance and skip and jump and spin in delight; I give thanks to the Lord for He is good; for His lovingkindness is everlasting (Psalm 118:1).

One day I sat in the car with a friend and she said to me, 'Talitha – it's not green, it's GREEN.' Kathy, you're right! It's so green, so lush, so very, very blooming, life-giving green!

Yes! There will be an abundance of flowers and singing and joy! The deserts will become as green as the mountains of Lebanon (Isaiah 35:2).

In His delight and my delight in Him my desert had become green. 'In Him I am a garden bursting into life.'

I will sing to the one I love a song! (Isaiah 5:1).

Twinkle toes singing, dancing to the one I love a love song – yes! I am even singing in the rain!

Pure Elegance

the meeting
Style: you've either got it or you ain't!

And she's got it- not a droplet but an overflow! Yes! Heather and her home are bursting at the seams with oodles of the stuff – real classy as my husband would say, with his broad Northern Irish accent and scruffy jeans.

My first visit with Heather was spent with me walking around her house, jaw hanging down and eyes bulging wide open as every room was a visual feast.

At one point I found myself stroking the wallpaper like it was some exotic pet. Eventually I had to keep my hands tucked in my pockets, as I just wanted to touch everything. There was so much attention to detail, with each element of colour, shape, balance, texture and lighting harmoniously woven together in the design.

My intention was to pop in for a quick nose around Heather's house, have a cup of tea and hopefully a nice biscuit and then slip home. Umm! I was having so much fun that the 1- hour slot in my diary soon became an afternoon of chatter, prayer and laughter.

As one who likes her grub, I was delighted when out came homemade leek and potato soup with a large chunk of wheaten bread – presented in a manner fit for a queen! Swanky white crockery, I thought to myself. Wow! Even the seasoned butter had its own tiny little bowl perched to the side of some highly decorative, edible garnish.

Yum! I was full but managed to indulge myself and squeeze in a couple of luxuriously rich chocolates washed down with freshly ground coffee.

I could even see my reflection in the highly polished sugar spoons - a novelty to me. The spoons in my house are dull and tea-stained – just one of those jobs I have never got round to!

My attention was brought back again, as my ears perked up hearing Heather reminisce about her days as a young girl when she retrieved little cracked jugs and cups from the wares that her father had brought home from an auction.

Once again they were valued, and with a handful of carefully arranged picked flowers were placed in her bright yellow bedroom at an angle where no cracks could be viewed. Even now as a grown woman, wife and mother of two university students, Heather has an eye and a heart to revamp the old or discarded and with her creative flair to bring a new lease of life to the drab and dreary - like she had for me on this dreary, cold, dark day.

My day had been turned upside down, and leaving Heather's house I was eager to return with Steve the photographer to photo-shoot the home – if she agreed. And I hoped she would, as she obviously did.

the photo-shoot

It was like an action-replay - only this time it was Steve's jaw that was dropping and his hand sliding along the textured paper and array of fabrics. Actually I found the whole thing highly entertaining. He was a happy chap, snapping away with the camera, quite obviously inspired by the surroundings and the smell of an apple pie baking in the oven - hopefully his reward for a hard day's work.

Yes - it was lunch and what amazing tucker we had. Presented like an artist's masterpiece - baked croissant with cheese, Parma ham, pepperoni and sun dried tomatoes. Then what Steve and I had been waiting for – out came the hot apple pie and sweet smelling custard. We were full and it was taking everything to get our butts off the comfortable farmhouse chairs away from the heat of the Rayburn cooker. 'Motivation, 1,2,3! Come on Steve we need to get working,' I said. But with that our coffee cups were refilled by Heather and some Italian biscuits appeared - apparently they had been hidden in a cupboard under lock and key, away from her husband.

the interview

By this time, Heather was no stranger – what with our first meeting and guided tour of her home, a photo-shoot and ongoing conversations! By the time of the interview I was meeting with a close friend.

The interview took place in a bustling coffee shop in Belfast. Again I had allocated a 1hour slot in my diary, desperately trying to be professional and focussed. Heather arrived on time and hugged me tight like at a family reunion. Within ten minutes it was obvious to me that this was going to be no punchy, quick interview and my well-planned schedule got thrown out of the window. It was time to unwind, embrace the moment and enjoy girlie time - and what an absolute hoot we had. Actually we laughed so much that we forgot ourselves, and with tears tripping down our faces suddenly realised that we had become the local entertainment. I looked like a panda, as my eyeliner and mascara had smudged together with streams of laughter.

Pure Elegance

Armed with my laptop, a cappuccino and a naughty slice of (Yes - you've guessed it!) chocolate cake, the interview began. My nimble little fingers struggled to keep up with Heather's stories of her Christian walk, and the highs and lows of being a self employed interior designer as well as project managing the construction and decoration or her own home.

I thought that I was a chatterbox, but I had certainly met my match. Time slipped by quickly as we talked about the workshops she ran for local Churches. Heather always accompanied talking about Jesus with a flower display or an interior design lesson.

I asked Heather how she became an interior designer, and very openly she shared how she had received no formal training but that others had recognised her gift before she had. What started as a hobby became her career, as she totally relied upon God to open the doors and inspire her. To be creative she looked to the creator - the one who threw the stars into space and decided the colour of the grass, the sky, the sea, the world and the universe. 'I believe a Christian's faith should be shared and in a constant state of evolving, listening, learning and developing,' she said, stirring her cup of coffee.

Even though Heather has designed very modern interiors, she chose to style her own home with a timeless elegance, cutting through the latest changing fads and trends. To me as an outsider, the timelessness of each room reminded me of an eternal perspective and how God is the beginning and the end. When in the home, I found myself meditating upon the scripture 'Be still and know that I am God.'

I could see more and more red and green lines on my screen, highlighting my spelling mistakes and bad punctuation. By this time my fingers were running more and more behind her flow of words, as she shared with me that the house to her is now a place of stillness, and recently a place for restoration as she has had to come to terms with the loss of both her parents in the past year. For her Psalm 23: 'He leads me besides still waters and restores my soul' is a living reality, hope and comfort.

Talking about home is so very personal; more and more I see how it's not about the four walls of a house, but about the experiences within the walls. At that moment words could not even begin to describe the intricate heart surgery that took place within the heart and the home. I was honoured to have shared the silence and memory.

The mood changed in a split second from being almost solemn and respectful to a joyful 'now.' An interior must relate to the requirements of the homeowner. 'For some it's a chewed kilim,' 'A what?' I said, not having the faintest notion of what she was talking about. All I could picture was a camel chomping on something. She looked at me. 'That's a rug,' she spluttered out between her shrieks of laughter at my ignorance! I got it; we are all different, with different tastes and needs. For some it's a bare wooden floor and others carpet; for some a soft fabric chair, for others a hard leather. I nodded, agreeing that in theory that's what a good interior designer needs to encourage and sometimes draw out of the client.

'There are so many elements and objects available these days, it means that we can have access to whatever makes us feel comfortable in our homes,' said Heather, who is often commissioned to source products for her customers.

'This is our 5th home - I planned it totally on graph paper and gave it to the architect to work out the stresses for the roof,' she said chomping on half of my piece of cake. I didn't have a clue what stresses meant, I think it's to do with the distribution of weight, but I was not about to ask.

Over the years, Heather had gathered a collection of ideas from magazine cut outs and books. With an assortment of thoughts scribbled on tattered paper, she embarked on bringing to fruition her dream home.

When walking around the house foundations, Heather's heart started racing - the rooms seemed smaller than she had imagined. Left wondering if she had made a mistake and got the sizes wrong, she was relieved as, brick by brick, the walls took on their own life. Now finished, with 18 rooms that are big and airy, it has provided ample space for Heather's creative ideas to flow in abundance.

'We found the land, sold our house and moved into temporary accommodation. The house we rented was so small and was piled high with both the landlord's furniture and ours,' said Heather, with a sigh of relief that those days were over.

One year later and ankle deep in sawdust, Heather and her family moved into the newly built home. A Formica table, a plastic dish and a fridge were all that accompanied them. After 11 years the house has evolved into a place of luxurious comfort. Memories of hand painting a kitchen by lamplight, and years with no curtains and carpets make the finished home a place to be appreciated and enjoyed all the more.

No clutter

There is no clutter in this house, unlike my own. Heather only likes to keep things that make a statement or are of use. When she sold the last house, she found a chunk of metal and threw it away. Too late she realised that she had thrown out the weight that regulated the pendulum in the grandfather clock. Now she thinks twice before having a ruthless clear-out session.

It was time for another coffee and (oh well – yes!) another piece of cake, seeing as I shared the last one. 'Heather,' I asked, 'you still have no clutter; I mean where do you keep things like slippers, cd's and books?' I nearly choked as she chuckled, proudly confessing that her slippers were stored in a food hamper in the hallway. 'Where else? 'Good one,' I said. 'Now I know that you are normal after all!' I can say this because I store my cutlery in an old bread-bin! After bribing her with a bite of my cake, she told me that the cds were carefully hidden away in an old leather case under the couch, and the books were in a shelving area under the stairs. 'That's not forgetting the spare bulbs in the pharmacy chest on the landing and the hidden chocolate biscuits under lock and key in the armoire,' she smiled. 'How do you spell that?' I exclaimed. 'I don't know - armwar, no armwour, ummm armware,' she replied. We both gave up, admiring the photo instead, and composing ourselves after drawing so much attention with our laughter and confessions of bad spelling!

The hall can create an amazing first impression. With light, airy, 'melt-in-the-mouth,' buttery colours, soft furnishings, deep windowsills, tile and marble, you would think you are walking into some stylish hotel only there's not a porter to meet you at the door.

This room is a place to be spoilt with a visual feast of lovely things, including Victorian braids and trims, sepia-toned old china, storm lanterns, a Venetian mask, a glossy black and gold tea box, a set of opera glasses and beautiful furnishings.

The drawing room is elegant with its strong French influence.

'Be still and know that I am God.'

"Armwar, no armwour, no armoire?"

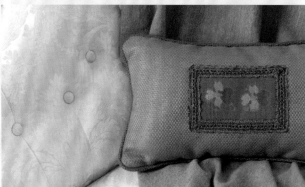

Two tapestries flank either side of the open fireplace. The room is calm, serene and tranquil.

The dining room

with its warm and inviting tones is home to a stunning concave bookcase full of crockery, custard cups and glass from many different periods. A Victorian table is surrounded by new, bespoke, high-backed, leather chairs that were purchased from England.

They were brought across the water jammed in the back of an old Volvo estate!

When she sold the last house, she found a chunk of metal and threw it away.

When it was too late, she realised that she had thrown out the weight that regulated the pendulum in the grandfather clock.

The kitchen reflects the heart of the house. The spiral staircase eventually (after 5 years) replaced an old pine ladder that led to the loft room and balcony overlooking the small walled garden and stables.

By using clippings from a roll of wallpaper artistically applied to the wall and enhanced by a glaze, Heather created a stunning bespoke finish in the pantry style porch at the back door.

Heather: your.space@inbox.com

'Yummie! Hot apple pie & custard!'

I love the roughness of the crates, which are both functional and decorative for fresh produce.

& FILS

es et Potagères

The long, wooden
tool that now
proudly hangs
on the kitchen
wall was a
holiday souvenir -
once used for
making rugs in
Croatia. This was
Heather's special
find - it was hidden
in a little shop,
beside a makeshift
counter and
underneath a
sleeping cat.

Watercress
flourishes
in a petite
flowerpot from
Amsterdam.

The sliding
wooden
doors lead
to a utility
area.

Simply delightful is the hand-painted chest of drawers, with its exquisite rich colours and design

The grand landing with its open staircase
and elegant banister is home to a beautiful,
ornate, French mirror that once belonged
to screening in a French lounge area,
and now reflects Irish light.

*The master bedroom is home
to a collection of gents'
travel scent bottles.*

The teddy called Wheaten was a gift from Heather's Dad who liked wheaten bread. Wheaten enjoys sitting on the banana - coloured loose covered sofa.

A dolls' house takes centre stage in Heather's daughter's room, waiting to be enjoyed upon her return from university. It was purchased as an investment many years ago. The collection of bespoke, handcrafted furniture has been added to over the years, and the story around the dolls' house has evolved including characters of Hanna the girl, Morag the maid and the father serving in India with his wife.

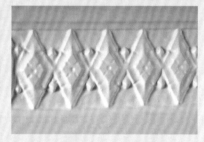

A French - feel bathroom, with its claw foot reproduction bath and hand painted marbled exterior, is both elegant and snug.

An unusual little corner sofa bought from an antique shop and reupholstered gives the room quite a regal feel.

photography: steven thompson - www.stevethompsonphotography.co.uk

Vintage Glamour

Roses and sprayed twigs are festooned with jewels

GEMS, BROOCHES, DIAMONDS, PEARLS
SPARKLY, GLITZY, GLAM, GIRLS.

Bling-it:

RAID
your jewellery box and untangle those old broken necklaces, odd earrings and brooches with missing jewels.

RACE
around the house and empty dishes and drawers to find that old broken bracelet from Aunt Molly.

RUMMAGE
deep into your handbag and see if any little sparkly gems are lurking in the crease of the lining.

Bling-it:

REVIVE
a dull looking or chipped vase with a draped broken necklace or selection of odd earrings.

REFLECT
the true glamorous you with some bling and make a simple carnation look a million dollars.

RADIATE
your heart of generosity with a surprise glitzy bouquet for a friend.

Carnations are back!

Full and frilly in pale pastels or two-colour varieties.

Roses

there's no glamour or luxury without roses; try dark reds
almost black to add a
touch of decadence as well as pastel shades.

Polianthes

more often known as tuber rose; fragrant and beautiful
for winter arrangements.

Moth orchids (Phalaenopsis)

lovely trailing stems of exotic orchids
to embrace the luxurious elem

Pretty, delicate Lisianthus

their pastel shades and delicate fullness
are perfect.

Kangaroo Paws

real name Anigozanthos, exotic, unusual and
velvety flowers.

Illusion Roses, white Roses
and pink edged
white Ranunculus
are tied together
to make a full bouquet.
Ribbons, pearls and filigree pins
are added to give a
vintage and glamorous look.

A glamorous collection of exotic orchids, roses and carnations
are seen through a curtain of pearls and crystals.

Illusion roses have been circled by a wreath of Lisianthus, twigs and then
fluffy white feathers. The whole bouquet has been delicately sprayed
with silver paint to give a frosted effect.

Jet black beads and black voile ribbon add a vintage look.

Flowers: Carnations, Lisianthus, Ranunculus and moth orchids are tied into small bunches with ribbons and decorated with pendants and brooches.

A luxurious cream rose surrounded by a collar of pearls.

artwork: lynsay spence, www.whitenoisestudios.com

in him we live, move

'For in Him we live and move and have our being,' I say as I pace around the room, with excitement welling up within my heart. 'For in Him we live and move and have our being' – my strides becoming larger and my arms swinging around in circles into the open universe, aware of the words IN HIM, mulling over my thoughts and speaking them out – 'In, innermost, inside, within Him, we live and move and have our being' (Acts 17:28).

By this time my squeaky floorboards are singing along with me, 'In Him, within Him, within God, we live!'

Because of who Jesus is and what he has done, my relationship with Him allows me to share in all His benefits and riches. He has given us the keys to His palace, and said, 'Make yourself at home. You see all this – it's all yours!'

Praise be to the God and Father of our Lord Jesus Christ, who has blessed us in the heavenly realms with every spiritual blessing in Christ (Ephesians 1:3).

Jesus is everything and has given us everything.

The earth is the Lord's and all it contains, The world and those who dwell in it (Psalm 24).

God is everywhere; everything is God's; He is always present; He indwells us and we walk drenched in His glory. 'Where can I go from your presence, oh Lord?' (Psalm 139:7). In Him we live in fullness!

design by www.markflint.net

and have our being

The fuller Greek meaning of the word live stems from the word Zoë – In Him we have life, we 'be' alive. And our very existence is from God. In Him we are alive spiritually and eternally together. In Him we are quickened, causing us to live. In Him we live in His righteousness and holiness through Jesus. In Him we live in the spirit. In Him we are new creations.

In Him – within God, we live and we move.

To move, shake, stir-up, to be moved, to be aroused. Arouse means to evoke or elicit (a reaction, emotion, or response), stimulate, to awaken from sleep. In God we are moved – we are awakened from sleep. We are awakened in love and affection.

God is moved by His love for us, causing Him to rejoice over us with singing. He will rejoice over you with singing (Zephaniah 3:17). God is spinning, dancing and rejoicing over us under the influence of His emotion of love for us.

The Lord your God is in the midst of you (Zephaniah 3:17). God is in the midst of us – the centre of us, and in Him we live and move and have our being.

In the midst of us, in Him; in the midst of us, in Him.

We awake.
We respond.
We 'are' – we have our being.

In Him and with Him we should rejoice, sing, dance and make noise – as on a day of festival – because He moves us, He arouses us with His love.

Like the Psalmist we can give thanks to the Lord for God is good; for His lovingkindness is everlasting (Psalm 118:1).

in him we live, move

The Lord is my strength and song, and He has become my salvation (Psalm 118:14).

God is my stronghold and He has become my salvation. In the Hebrew the word 'become' means to exist, to breathe, to come to pass, and it is dynamic.

God is active.
God breathes life into us.

For in Him all the whole fullness of Deity (the Godhead) continues to dwell in bodily form [giving complete expression of the divine nature]. And you are in Him, made full and having come to fullness of life [in Christ you too are filled with the Godhead – Father, Son and Holy Spirit and reach full spiritual stature. And He is the Head [of every angelic principality and power] (Colossians 2:9,10 Amp).

In Christ,
we are full,
we are loaded.

For God did not give us a spirit of timidity, but a spirit of power, of love and of self-discipline (2 Timothy 1:7). We have the 'dunamis,' dynamite power of God indwelling us!

How can I repay the Lord
For all his goodness to me?
I will lift the cup of salvation
And call on the name of the Lord
(Psalm 116:12,13 NIV).

How can I lift up, accept, carry, marry, magnify, wear and yield to the cup of salvation? Shouts of joy and victory resound in the tents of the righteous (Psalm 118:15).

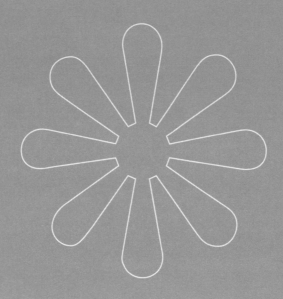

and have our being

Shouts of joy and victory resound in the lives, the HOMES, the marriages, the families, the workplace, the churches of the righteous, for we are LIVING STONES!

I shall be sure and allow the light – the morning star to arise in my heart (2 Peter 1:19).

I shall live in the fullness of His love.

Love the Lord your God with all your heart and with all your soul and with all your mind. This is the first and greatest commandment. And the second is like it: Love your neighbour as yourself (Matthew 22:37).

We can say Jesus love in our hearts, we can think Jesus love in our minds and we can speak Jesus love with our mouths into existence in the lives of others.

My life shall be His worship.

For he chose us in him before the creation of the world to be holy and blameless in his sight. In love he predestined us to be adopted as his sons through Jesus Christ, in accordance with his pleasure and will – to the praise of his glorious grace, which he has freely given us in the one he loves (Ephesians 1:4).

In God I shall live and move and have my being.

in him we live, move

Delighting in the fullness of who God is (Isaiah 61:10); delighting in fullness of the Word of God (Romans 8:23); delighting in the fullness of the works of God (1 Samuel 2:1); delighting in the fullness of God delighting and enjoying us.

And now I am coming to you; I say these things while I am still in the world, so that My joy may be made full and complete and perfect in them [that they may experience My delight fulfilled in them, that My enjoyment may be perfected in their souls, that they may have My gladness within them, filling their hearts (John 17:13).

I will lift the cup of salvation by living in the reality and the fullness of God's delight in me and my delight in Him.

But may all who search for you be filled with joy and gladness. May those who love your salvation repeatedly shout, 'The Lord is great' (Psalm 40:16).

In Jesus we can shout, 'The Lord is great'. As we shout, God dances in delight with shouts of joy for us. He will dance with shouts of joy for you (Zephaniah 3:17).

Smiling inside, we live, sleep, eat, drink, breathe the love of God in our hearts, our thoughts, our feelings, our everything.

Then like Paul and Silas we can sing to God, even if it feels like we are in a prison and our feet in are in the stocks.

About midnight Paul and Silas were praying and singing hymns to God, and the other prisoners were listening to them (Acts 16:25).

and have our being

We can give thanks to the Lord for He is good; For His lovingkindness is everlasting (Psalm 118:1).

Smiling inside because our God is good, we can have twinkle toes dancing, gladness within and 'singing and dancing in the rain'!

God adopts us, blesses us, cares for us, delights in us, encourages us, forgives us, shows us grace, heals us, gives us insight, gives us joy. God is kindness, God is love, God is mercy. God gives us newness, God gives us opportunities. He is our peace; He give us quietness; He is our refuge and salvation. God is truth, He is unchangeable. God is our victory; God is our wholeness; God makes our Yoke easy and burden light, and God is our zeal.

May the Lord bless you and keep you; may the Lord make his face to shine upon you, and be gracious to you; may the Lord lift up His countenance upon you,and give you peace (Numbers 6:24).

P.S. to me, to you, a note in my journal

Today I sit with a half-empty house. God said to sell it, and we have and so very quickly. Yesterday a queue of people arrived at the door and took, what caught their eye. They kept asking if I was sad, and I said 'No' because I am not; I am excited. Most of the furniture and ornaments are gone, and the rooms and walls are bare.

I had a fancy sledge bed. Tonight I am sleeping on an inflatable lilo. It feels great all this. I feel so free, so uncluttered by all that stuff: funny this, this life, this journey. Right now we don't even know where we are going to live. Sam and I keep laughing, saying God will show us when we need to know.

Today I have also finished the bookazine; funny that, too. It all started here; the house, Sam, living stones. I wonder what's next; what an adventure!

You, me, in Him, living stones. A kiss to God, a kiss to Sam, a kiss x to you!

Tali x x x